Short Scenes
from
SHAKESPEARE

Nineteen Cuttings for the Classroom

by
Samuel Selden

Edited by
William-Alan Landes

PLAYERS PRESS, Inc.
P.O. Box 1132
Studio City, CA 91614-0132

SHORT SCENES FROM SHAKESPEARE
© Copyright , 1993, by William-Alan Landes
ISBN 0-88734-632-4
Library of Congress Catalog Number: 93-4582

PLAYERS PRESS, Inc.
P.O. Box 1132
Studio City, CA 91614-0132, U.S.A.

Library of Congress Cataloging-in-Publication Data

Shakespeare, William, 1564-1616.
    Short scenes from Shakespeare / edited and preface by William-Alan
Landes.
        p.   cm.
    ISBN 0-88734-632-4
    1. Monologues.   2. Dialogues.   I. Landes, William-Alan.   II.
Title.
PR2774.L36   1993
822.3'3--dc20   93-4582
                                                              CIP

Simultaneously Published
U.S.A., U.K., Canada and Australia

Printed in the U.S.A.

PREFACE

This collection of duologues and monologues from Shakespeare's plays has a two-fold purpose: first, to provide material for short presentations and auditions; and second, to give students, of acting ad directing, an easy to use, but interesting, selection for practice work. We have prepared this book with the hope that working with this material will aid in exploring the entertainment values and poetic beauty of Shakespeare's plays. We have tried to suggest how the performer needs to present this material in order to express the essential elements of these works. The staging plans are simply designed. Costumes, sets and properties are also limited to the barest needs. Our concept was to place the emphasis on the actor, but if a more elaborate presentation is needed, these works can be dressed, set and grouped together to make an interesting theatrical presentation.

We acknowledge appreciatively the fact that the text used in this selection is based on *The Complete Plays and Poems of William Shakespeare*, edited by William Allan Neilson and Charles Jarvis Hiel. In addition, we have borrowed some of the excellent notes, explaining certain words and expressions. We have not edited Shakespeare but have, to facilitate performance, modified some of the punctuation.

TABLE OF CONTENTS

HOW TO USE THIS BOOK

The scenes that follow are arranged for easy staging on an open platform or at one end of a classroom. Little floor space is needed for any of them. For simplicity of staging, all of the entrances and exits for the characters in these selections are placed at the right and left only. With the exception of one or two scenes which seem to need a more specific environment, no scenery is indicated. The furniture is limited to tables and chairs, and the number of hand properties has been held to a bare minimum.

Although no period costumes have been called for, the director can quite appropriately put his actors into historic dress if he wishes to give the scenes more of a Shakespearean flavor. Decoration of the action in any way, however, is not required; the emphasis throughout this book is directed straight toward the player's performance.

In the suites of scenes, such as those from *Romeo and Juliet*, and *Macbeth*, there is a sequence. A person working out a program can respect this order, or he can disregard it; he can pick and choose among the several selections in the book and put together scenes of a kind, or scenes of very different kind - such as solo, duologue and group passages, or comedy and serious bits - to fit whatever plan he has in mind.

Each scene is preceded by a brief introduction which sketches the dramatic setting for what follows. This may be spoken by one of the performers, or by someone picked from outside the cast. If four or five scenes are to be presented together in one program, it might be wise to appoint for the occasion a Master of Ceremonies who would introduce the series as a whole, then speak, or read, the introductions to the individual scenes.

It will be noted that the introduction to the first scene in a group from one play, such as *Romeo and Juliet* or the *Macbeth* sequence, is made a little longer than those that follow since it has to sketch in some of the background facts for the group as a whole. In a program in which a scene with a short introduction is picked out of the group the Master of Ceremonies can, of course, borrow a sentence or two from the longer introduction to fill out whatever additional information seems to be necessary for a full understanding of the scene being used.

Each scene in this book has been given a tentative title just so that it will have a dramatic banner. The title comes from no traditional naming of the selection. Actors and directors should feel quite free to substitute another title or, if they wish, to omit the title altogether.

A Note on the Stage Directions

In conformity with stage conventions "right" and "left" in the directions for movement are related to the point of view of the actor looking toward the audience - Stage Right or Stage Left. That is, "right" is the audience's left, and "left" the audience's right. "Down stage," or "below," is toward the footlights, or the front of the platform; "up stage" is in the opposite direction. "Off" means beyond the visible part of the acting area, usually to the right or the left.

ON THE ACTING OF SHAKESPEARE

Those who approach the acting oShakespeare's plays for the first time usually find it difficult. This is quite understandable. No one should be ashamed to admit it. The plays were written more than three hundred years ago and the Elizabethan English which Shakespeare spoke naturally then is somewhat different from what we use today. Also, the rhythm of the blank verse which Shakespeare employed for poetic and dramatic purposes makes many of his sentences, already strange with respect to vocabulary, seem even more strange to our ears.

Fortunately, a little experience in the reading of Shakespeare's dialogue reveals that the differences between his expressions of thought and ours are superficial rather than fundamental. The inner matter of what he is trying to say about the love, hatred, fear, and wonder of people is just as modern as it is Elizabethan, and the forms of his communication of this become both logical and readily understandable for us as soon as we get a little more accustomed to the sound of expressions.

The first thing that the beginning player should do, of course, is to make sure that he does understand every part of what he is preparing to interpret. As he studies his role the actor should make certain that he is not just guessing at meanings. He should check carefully the editor's notes, and if he still has trouble catching onto the meaning of certain phrases, such as those for example that make reference to mythological or historical personages not known to him, he should ask his director to explain them to him.

One of the best aids to getting at meaning is to read the lines to oneself with special attention to the meter. The accents fall in certain places, and these points of natural emphasis often show where are the important key words. Frequently, the accenting of just one word in this way will unlock the secret of a whole line which has hitherto resisted every other kind of penetration.

When the time comes for the actor to render a passage out loud let him do it with courage. There is nothing sacred about a printed page; Shakespeare wrote his pieces first of all to be *acted*. A few mistakes at the beginning, even bad ones, won't really matter in the end. The player should have the courage to try once, then try again. Probably the wisest way to go about the rendering of Elizabethan blank verse is to do it in three steps:

(1) Read the part through once or twice out loud to get the general drift of the thought, the character and the poetic sound in it.

(2) Now analyze it carefully phrase by phrase to be sure that you have all the meanings and have effectively modeled all the various vocal elements of the interpretation for the release of these meanings.

(3) Put the pieces together again and work for ease of utterance and poetic pace.

Beginning actors tend to make one of three mistakes: they read Shakespeare too rapidly, or too slowly (this is more common), or they deliver every line as if it were a part of a pompous political speech. Some of Shakespeare's characters, such as the Prince of Morocco, speak pompously (on occasion). Juliet's lines, however, should be very light, very simple, very natural, since she is never anything but a young unsophisticated girl.

Blank verse is poetry. This does not mean, however, that the speaking of it should have a heavy falling of the voice at the end of each line. Many of Shakespeare's sentences extend over two or three lines then end perhaps in the middle of the next line. Here is an example:

> ...I have heard
> That guilty creatures sitting at a play
> Have by the very cunning of the scene
> Been struck so to the soul that presently
> They have proclaimed their malefactions;
> For murder, though it hath no tongue, will speak
> With most miraculous organ. I'll have these players
> Play something like....

Such a sentence as the first one here should be read as any other kind of sentence, that is with a pause for breath if it is needed at one of the commas or semicolon points, but with no final dropping of the voice till one gets to the end of the sentence. The following sentence should begin easily with a new breath even though the first word of it is in the middle of the line.

What Shakespeare has to say must be delivered sensuously and actively, with great variation of pitch, force, and quality of tone. The variety is demanded, not because this makes the rendition more authentically Elizabethan, but because all the changes of voice have to be used to give full expression to the meaning. Shakespeare conveys most of his thought and emotion through the form of imagery. This cannot be created, however hard one tries, with a flat voice. The actor must perform with a live, vibrant body, with all his senses alert to the sights and sounds around him, especially those pertaining to the human presences near him, and he should speak in such a way as to show how all these influences are affecting him sensuously, thoughtfully and emotionally as the drama progresses.

Listening to experienced actors play Shakespeare is very helpful. If one is situated where one cannot attend professional productions, one can listen to some of the excellent recordings now available. The young actor should use these as dramatic and poetic guides only, and not become obsessed by a desire to imitate the external sounds or accents. These accents or sounds have nothing to add to a good interpretation and may, in fact, be a hindrance to audience appreciation. There are many excellent British, American, Australian and Canadian Shakespearean actors; and many foreign actors that do not perform in English.

An excellent handbook, that the serious performer should read, is *SHAKESPEARE SOUNDED SOUNDLY.* It will help in understanding Shakespeare's language and improve the useage of his verse.

Samuel Selden
and
William-Alan Landes

THE

SCENES

A FORBIDDEN VISIT

Romeo and Juliet. act II, scene 2

ROMEO

JULIET

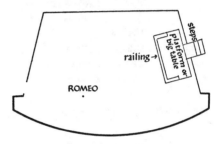

In the orchard, below the balcony
of the Capulet home in Verona

INTRODUCTION. Two prominent families of Verona, the Montagues and the Capulets, hate each other bitterly. The feuding has become so intense that men have fought and killed each other in the streets, and the Prince has found it necessary to order the brawls to cease under penalty of death. But love pays little heed to family quarrels. Romeo, son of the Montagues, and Juliet, daughter of the Capulets, have met at a ball and secretly lost their hearts to each other,

3

though neither yet knows the other's feeling. Now it is later that same night. Juliet in her room has been unable to sleep for thinking of Romeo. Determined to see her, Romeo has eluded his friends, climbed over the wall of the Capulets' orchard garden, and is standing in the shadow below the balcony of Juliet's room.

> [*Romeo, standing at the right, looks off stage in the direction of his departing friends, but the remark is to himself.*]

ROMEO
He jests at scars who never felt a wound.
> [*He turns and sees the light come on the balcony at the left. He speaks softly to himself.*]

But, soft! what light through yonder window
  breaks?
> [*Juliet comes quietly out onto the balcony. Romeo's breath catches as he gazes at her.*]

It is the east, and Juliet is the sun.
Arise, fair sun, and kill the envious moon,
Who is already sick and pale with grief
That thou, her maid, art far more fair than she.
Be not her maid, since she is envious;
Her vestal livery is but sick and green,
And none but fools do wear it; cast it off.
> [*She turns and looks out into the garden. Romeo's heart beats faster.*]

It is my lady, O, it is my love!
O that she knew she were!

*[Juliet's lips move, but he cannot hear
what she is whispering to herself—prob-
ably something about her memory of
Romeo.]*
She speaks, yet she says nothing; what of that?
Her eye discourses; I will answer it.
             [He steps forward, but hesitates.]
I am too bold, 'tis not to me she speaks.
Two of the fairest stars in all the heaven,
Having some business, do entreat her eyes
To twinkle in their spheres till they return.
What if her eyes were there, they in her head?
The brightness of her cheek would shame those
       stars,
As daylight doth a lamp; her eyes in heaven
Would through the airy region stream so bright
That birds would sing and think it were not night.
             *[Juliet puts her hand to her cheeks, still
             thinking of Romeo, doubtlessly.]*
See, how she leans her cheek upon her hand!
O, that I were a glove upon that hand,
That I might touch that cheek!

             JULIET
             [Speaking for the first time out loud.]
                                    Ay me!

             ROMEO
             [Still to himself]
                                    She speaks!
O, speak again, bright angel! for thou art
As glorious to this night, being o'er my head,

As is a winged messenger of heaven
Unto the white-upturned wond'ring eyes
Of mortals that fall back to gaze on him
When he bestrides the lazy-pacing clouds
And sails upon the bosom of the air.

JULIET
O Romeo, Romeo! wherefore art thou Romeo?
        [*Being Romeo makes him a Montague
        and therefore an enemy, alas.*]
Deny thy father and refuse thy name;
Or, if thou wilt not, be but sworn my love,
And I'll no longer be a Capulet.

ROMEO
Shall I hear more, or shall I speak at this?

JULIET
'Tis but thy name that is my enemy;
Thou art thyself, though not a Montague.
        [*You would be very much yourself, even
        if you weren't a Montague.*]
What's Montague? It is nor hand, nor foot,
Nor arm, nor face, nor any other part
Belonging to a man. O, be some other name!
What's in a name? That which we call a rose
By any other word would smell as sweet;
So Romeo would, were he not Romeo call'd,
Retain that dear perfection which he owes*
Without that title. Romeo, doff thy name,
And for thy name, which is no part of thee,
Take all myself.

* *owes:* possesses

ROMEO
[*Now he steps forward and speaks out loud
enough for to hear him—but not so loud
as to wake the other people in the house.*]
        I take thee at thy word.
Call me but love, and I'll be new baptiz'd;
Henceforth I never will be Romeo.

JULIET
[*Frightened.*]
What man art thou that thus bescreen'd in night
So stumblest on my counsel?*

ROMEO   By a name
I know not how to tell thee who I am.
My name, dear saint, is hateful to myself,
Because it is an enemy to thee;
Had I it written, I would tear the word.

JULIET
[*Suddenly hopeful, but still scarcely be-
lieving that this could really be Romeo!*]
My ears have yet not drunk a hundred words
Of thy tongue's uttering, yet I know the sound.
Art thou not Romeo, and a Montague?

ROMEO
Neither, fair maid, if either thee dislike.†

JULIET
How cam'st thou hither, tell me, and wherefore?
The orchard walls are high and hard to climb,

* *counsel:* secret   † *dislike:* displeases

And the place death, considering who thou art,
If any of my kinsmen find thee here.

ROMEO
[*Joking lightly.*]
With love's light wings did I o'erperch these walls;
For stony limits cannot hold love out,
And what love can do, that dares love attempt;
Therefore thy kinsmen are no stop to me.*

JULIET
[*Fearful for Romeo's safety.*]
If they do see thee, they will murder thee.

ROMEO
Alack, there lies more peril in thine eye
Than twenty of their swords! Look thou but sweet,
And I am proof against their enmity.

JULIET
I would not for the world they saw thee here.

ROMEO
I have night's cloak to hide me from their eyes;†
And but thou love me, let them find me here.
My life were better ended by their hate,
Than death prorogued, wanting of thy love.‡

JULIET
[*She is willing to relax a little now and
flirt with this wonderful young man.*]
By whose direction found'st thou out this place?

---

* *stop:* hindrance † *night's cloak:* the darkness
‡ *prorogued:* postponed

ROMEO

By Love, that first did prompt me to inquire;
He lent me counsel and I lent him eyes.
I am no pilot; yet, wert thou as far
As that vast shore wash'd with the farthest sea,
I should adventure for such merchandise.

> [*He would be willing to go to the end of
> the world to find her.*]

JULIET

> [*Perhaps this is the first time she has had
> a compliment like this and she is very
> pleased.*]

Thou know'st the mask of night is on my face,
Else would a maiden blush bepaint my cheek
For that which thou has heard me speak to-night.
Fain would I dwell on form, fain, fain deny
What I have spoke; but farewell compliment!*

> [*Suddenly and impulsively, like the little
> girl she is.*]

Dost thou love me? I know thou wilt say ay,
And I will take thy word; yet, if thou swear'st,
Thou mayst prove false. At lovers' perjuries,
They say, Jove laughs. O gentle Romeo,

> [*She wants Romeo to say yes. But if he
> does, she will be afraid to trust him.*]

If thou dost love, pronounce it faithfully;†
Or if thou think'st I am too quickly won,

---

* *compliment:* convention
† *pronounce it faithfully:* say it in such a way as to make me
trust you

I'll frown and be perverse and say thee nay,
So thou wilt woo; but else, not for the world.
        *[She is beginning to realize that she has
        been behaving in a very unladylike way.]*
I should have been more strange, I must confess,*
But that thou overheard'st, ere I was ware,
My true love's passion; therefore pardon me,
And not impute this yielding to light love,†
Which the dark night hath so discovered.‡

        ROMEO
Lady, by yonder blessed moon I vow§
That tips with silver all these fruit-tree tops—

        JULIET
O, swear not by the moon, the inconstant moon,
That monthly changes in her circled orb,
Lest that thy love prove likewise variable.

        ROMEO
        [At a loss.]
What shall I swear by?

        JULIET
                Do not swear at all;
Or, if thou wilt, swear by thy gracious self,
Which is the god of my idolatry.**
And I'll believe thee.

        ROMEO
                If my heart's dear love—

---

* *strange:* reserved
† *impute this yielding to light love:* think of my easy response
as caused by a frivolous attitude   ‡ *discovered:* revealed
§ *vow:* swear ** *my idolatry:* everything I worship

JULIET
Well, do not swear. Although I joy in thee,
I have no joy of this contract tonight;*
It is too rash, too unadvis'd, too sudden,
Too like the lightning, which doth cease to be
Ere one can say it lightens.
           [She looks at him and smiles lovingly]
                Sweet, good night!
This bud of love, by summer's ripening breath,
May prove a beauteous flower when next we meet.
           [Leaning away over the balcony railing
           toward him.]
Good night, good night! as sweet repose and rest
Come to thy heart as that within my breast!

ROMEO
O, wilt thou leave me so unsatisfied?

JULIET
           [Giggling. Romeo makes love so beauti-
           fully.]
What satisfaction canst thou have tonight?

ROMEO
Th' exchange of thy love's faithful vow for mine.

JULIET
I gave thee mine before thou didst request it;
And yet I would it were to give again.

ROMEO
Wouldst thou withdraw it? For what purpose, love?

* *contract:* agreement

JULIET

But to be frank, and give it thee again.*
And yet I wish but for the thing I have.
My bounty is as boundless as the sea,
My love as deep; the more I give to thee,
The more I have, for both are infinite.

[*We hear Juliet's Nurse calling her, off
left.*]

I hear some noise within; dear love, adieu!

[*The Nurse calls again. Juliet calls back to
her, then whispers to Romeo.*]

Anon, good nurse! Sweet Montague, be true.
Stay but a little, I will come again.

[*This is to Romeo. She has no intention of
letting him leave quite yet. She goes into
her room, left.*]

ROMEO
[*Moving back toward the right, looking
out into the night.*]

O blessed, blessed night! I am afeard,
Being in night, all this is but a dream,
Too flattering-sweet to be substantial.

[*Juliet comes back onto the balcony.*]

JULIET

Three words, dear Romeo, and good night indeed.
If that thy bent of love be honorable,†
Thy purpose marriage, send me word tomorrow,
By one that I'll procure to come to thee,

* *frank:* generous   † *bent:* inclination

Where and what time thou wilt perform the rite;
And all my fortunes at thy foot I'll lay
And follow thee my lord throughout the world.

NURSE
[*Off left.*]
Madam!

JULIET
[*The first part to the Nurse, then turning
back to Romeo.*]
I come, anon.——But if thou mean'st not well,
I do beseech thee——

NURSE
Madam!

JULIET
[*To the Nurse.*]
By and by, I come:——
[*To Romeo.*]
To cease thy suit, and leave me to my grief.
Tomorrow will I send.

ROMEO
So thrive my soul——

JULIET
A thousand times good night!
[*Tossing him a kiss she goes into her
room.*]

ROMEO
A thousand times the worse, to want thy light.

Love goes toward love, as schoolboys from their
  books,
But love from love, toward school with heavy
  looks.
>   [*Not expecting to see Juliet again, he has
>   gone off into the darkness at the right.
>   But Juliet is back on the balcony!*]

JULIET
Hist! Romeo, hist! O, for a falconer's voice,
To lure this tassel-gentle back again!*
>   [*She can't see Romeo and is afraid he's
>   gone now.*]
Bondage is hoarse, and may not speak aloud;†
Else would I tear the cave where Echo lies,
And make her airy tongue more hoarse than mine,
With repetition of my Romeo's name.
Romeo!

ROMEO
[*Coming forward into the light.*]
  My dear?

JULIET
          What o'clock tomorrow
Shall I send to thee?

ROMEO
          By the hour of nine.

---

* *tassel-gentle:* pet hawk
† *bondage is hoarse:* the necessity for not waking the people
in the house makes me call quietly

JULIET
I will not fail; 'tis twenty year till then.
            [*She looks at him and giggles again.*]
I have forgot why I did call thee back.

ROMEO
            [*Smiling back up at her.*]
Let me stand here till thou remember it.

JULIET
I shall forget, to have thee still stand there,*
Rememb'ring how I love thy company.

ROMEO
And I'll still stay, to have thee still forget,
Forgetting any other home but this.

JULIET
            [*Being realistic now.*]
'Tis almost morning, I would have thee gone;
And yet no farther than a wanton's bird,
That lets it hop a little from her hand,
Like a poor prisoner in his twisted gyves,†
And with a silk thread plucks it back again,
So loving-jealous of his liberty.

ROMEO
I would I were thy bird.

JULIET   Sweet, so would I;

* *I shall forget, to...:* I'll make a point of forgetting, in order
to....   † *gyves:* fetters

Yet I should kill thee with much cherishing.
> [*But she must let him go so he won't get
> caught.*]

Good night, good night! Parting is such sweet sorrow,
That I shall say good night till it be morrow.
> [*Now she is gone finally.*]

ROMEO

Sleep dwell upon thine eyes, peace in thy breast!
Would I were sleep and peace, so sweet to rest!
> [*He goes off slowly to the right, walking
> as if he were in a daze—in which, of
> course, he is.*]

THE DATE

Romeo and Juliet. act II, scene 5

JULIET

HER NURSE

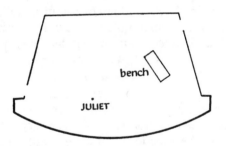

bench

JULIET

A corner of the Capulet garden

INTRODUCTION. The meeting in the orchard has confirmed the love of Romeo and Juliet. They are now trying to get married. Juliet has sent her Nurse to Romeo to find out from him just when and where they can arrange a wedding. She is pacing back and forth in a corner of the Capulet garden, waiting for the old woman's return.

JULIET

The clock struck nine when I did send the nurse;
In half an hour she promis'd to return.

> [*She tries to find some excuse for the
> Nurse's delay.*]

Perchance she cannot meet him: that's not so.

> [*It must be the old woman's physical con-
> dition.*]

O, she is lame! Love's heralds should be thoughts,
Which ten times faster glide than the sun's beams
Driving back shadows over louring hills;*
Therefore do nimble-pinion'd doves draw Love,
And therefore hath the wind-swift Cupid wings.

> [*She looks up at the sky, almost suffocated
> by her impatience.*]

Now is the sun upon the highmost hill
Of this day's journey, and from nine till twelve
Is three long hours, yet she is not come.
Had she affections and warm youthful blood,
She would be as swift in motion as a ball;

> [*Her voice is high and light as she thinks
> of the motion of the ball.*]

My words would bandy her to my sweet love,†
And his to me;

> [*Now her voice drops as if she were plod-
> ding slowly and wearily.*]

But old folks, marry, feign as they were dead,‡

---

* *louring:* scowling   † *bandy:* toss   ‡ *marry:* an interjection
meaning "indeed" or "to be sure"   *feign:* pretend

Unwieldy, slow, heavy and pale as lead.
> [*Juliet is now at the gate right. She catches
> sight of the approaching Nurse and her
> whole manner changes immediately.*]

O God, she comes!
> [*The Nurse enters and Juliet runs to her
> excitedly.*]
>   O honey nurse, what news?

Hast thou met with him?
> [*She hugs the old woman.*]

Now, good sweet nurse—

> [*The Nurse takes a step or two into the
> garden. To tease Juliet she puts on a dole-
> ful expression.*]
>   O Lord, why look'st thou sad?

Though news be sad, yet tell them merrily;
If good, thou sham'st the music of sweet news
By playing it to me with so sour a face.

NURSE
> [*Waddling over toward the bench left.*]

I am aweary, give me leave awhile.
Fie, how my bones ache! What a jaunce have I
  had!*

JULIET
I would thou hadst my bones, and I thy news.
> [*She hugs her again.*]

Nay, come, I pray thee, speak; good, good nurse,
  speak.

---

* *jaunce:* a tiring journey

NURSE
Jesu, what haste! Can you not stay awhile?
[*She collapses onto the bench.*]
Do you not see that I am out of breath?

JULIET
How art thou out of breath, when thou hast breath
To say to me that thou art out of breath?
Th' excuse that thou dost make in this delay
Is longer than the tale thou dost excuse.
[*Kneeling by the Nurse pleadingly.*]
Is thy news good, or bad? Answer to that;
Say either, and I'll stay the circumstance.*
Let me be satisfied, is't good or bad?

[*The old woman is greatly enjoying her
teasing of Juliet. She pretends to be thor-
oughly disgusted with the young girl's in-
fatuation with Romeo. While she seems to
be tearing him apart she is actually compli-
menting him.*]

NURSE
Well, you have made a simple† choice; you know
not how to choose a man. Romeo! no, not he.
Though his face be better than any man's, yet his
leg excels all men's; and for a hand, and a foot,
and a body, though they be not to be talk'd on, yet
they are past compare. He is not the flower of cour-
tesy,

* *stay the circumstance:* wait for the details
† *simple:* foolish

[*She remembers a somewhat unpleasant personal meeting with Romeo but she is willing to forgive him.*]

but, I'll warrant him, as gentle as a lamb.

[*Starting to get up.*]

Go thy ways, wench; serve God. What, have you din'd at home?

[*Juliet pulls her back down onto the bench.*]

NURSE

No, no! But all this did I know before.
What says he of our marriage? What of that?

NURSE

Lord, how my head aches! What a head have I!
It beats as it would fall in twenty pieces.

[*She puts a hand to her back. Juliet jumps up and starts to rub it for her.*]

My back o' t' other side,

[*Juliet rushes to the other side and rubs there.*]

O, my back, my back!
Beshrew your heart for sending me about
To catch my death with jauncing up and down!

JULIET

I' faith, I am sorry that thou art not well.

[*Kissing her.*]

Sweet, sweet, sweet nurse, tell me, what says my
  love?

[*Now the Nurse sounds as if she would
tell her.*]

NURSE

Your love says, like an honest* gentleman, and a
courteous, and a kind, and a handsome, and, I
warrant, a virtuous—
[*She suddenly turns to Juliet and asks in
a perfectly matter-of-fact voice.*]
Where is your mother?
[*Juliet jumps up exasperated.*]

JULIET

Where is my mother! Why, she is within;†
Where should she be? How oddly thou repliest!
"Your love says, like an honest gentleman,
'Where is your mother?' "

NURSE

O God's lady dear!
Are you so hot? Marry, come up, I trow;‡
Is this the poultice for my aching bones?
Henceforward do your messages yourself.
[*She turns away pettishly.*]

JULIET

Here's such a coil!§
[*Seizing the old woman and making her
face her.*]
Come, what says Romeo?

* *honest:* honorable   † *within:* inside the house
‡ *marry come up:* an expression of impatience   *I trow:* I
wonder   § *coil:* fuss

[*The Nurse pauses a moment, then smiles and drops her voice to a friendly whisper.*]

NURSE
Have you got leave to go to shrift today?

JULIET
I have.

NURSE
Then hie you hence to Friar Laurence' cell;
There stays a husband to make you a wife.
[*She looks affectionately at the young girl's blushing.*]
Now comes the wanton blood up in your cheeks;*
They'll be in scarlet straight at any news.†
Hie you to church; I must another way,
To fetch a ladder, by the which your love
Must climb a bird's nest soon when it is dark.
I am the drudge and toil in your delight,
But you shall bear the burden soon at night.
Go; I'll to dinner; hie you to the cell.
[*She goes out at the left while Juliet twirls happily on her toes.*]

JULIET
Hie to high fortune! Honest nurse, farewell.
[*She runs out the garden gate.*]

* *wanton:* wild   † *straight:* immediately

HONORABLE VILLAIN

Romeo and Juliet. act III, scene 2

JULIET

HER NURSE

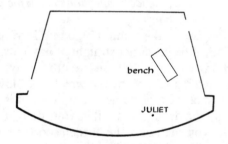

The Capulet garden

INTRODUCTION. Romeo and Juliet have been married secretly by a friendly monk, Friar Laurence, but they have not had an opportunity to be together since the ceremony. Juliet has sent her old Nurse back to Romeo to arrange a meeting, not knowing that since she saw him this morning he has become involved in a fight in the street and has killed Juliet's cousin, Tybalt. Once more we find Juliet in the garden, pacing back and forth impatiently.

24

JULIET
[*Looking out at the sky.*]
Gallop apace, you fiery-footed steeds,*
Toward Phoebus' lodging; such a wagoner†
As Phaeton would whip you to the west‡
And bring in cloudy night immediately.
> [*Turning toward the left, as if that is where
> the darkness will be coming from.*]
Spread thy close curtain, love-performing night,
That runaway's eyes may wink, and Romeo§
Leap to these arms untalk'd of and unseen!
Lovers can see to do their amorous rites
By their own beauties, or if love be blind,
It best agrees with night. Come, civil night,
> [*Looking longingly again in the direction
> of the approaching darkness.*]
Thou sober-suited matron, all in black,
And learn me how to lose a winning match,
Play'd for a pair of stainless maidenhoods.
Hood my unmann'd blood, bating in my cheeks,**
With thy black mantle, till strange love grow
    bold,††
Think true love acted simple modesty.

---

* *fiery-footed steeds:* the horses pulling the sun chariot across the sky
† *Phoebus' lodging:* the sun's resting place in the west
‡ *Phaeton:* the driver of the sun chariot
§ *runaway:* perhaps the sun, or the moon, or the stars
  wink: close
** *hood:* cover   *unmanned:* untamed   *bating:* fluttering
†† *strange:* new, strange, therefore shy

[*She looks once more in the direction of night, then moves over toward the gate through which she wishes she could see Romeo coming.*]

Come, night; come, Romeo; come, thou day in
    night;
For thou wilt lie upon the wings of night,
Whiter than new snow on a raven's back.
Come, gentle night, come, loving, black-brow'd
    night,
        [*She is begging with all her heart.*]
Give me my Romeo; and, when he shall die,
        [*Looking up into the sky lovingly.*]
Take him and cut him out in little stars,
And he will make the face of heaven so fine
That all the world will be in love with night
And pay no worship to the garish sun.
        [*She sighs and walks slowly to the left.*]
O, I have bought the mansion of a love,
But not possess'd it, and, though I am sold,
Not yet enjoy'd.
            [*Stamping her foot impatiently.*]
                So tedious is this day
As is the night before some festival
To an impatient child that hath new robes
And may not wear them.
            [*She sees the Nurse approaching down the path toward the gate right.*]
                    O, here comes my nurse,
And she brings news; and every tongue that speaks
But Romeo's name speaks heavenly eloquence.

[*The Nurse enters with a coiled up rope
and Juliet runs eagerly to her.*]
Now, nurse, what news? What hast thou there?
   The cords
That Romeo bid thee fetch?

NURSE   Ay, ay, the cords.
[*She throws the rope down. Then she begins to wring her hands.*]

JULIET
Ah me! what news? Why dost thou wring thy
   hands?

NURSE
[*Walking sorrowfully toward the left.*]
Ah, well-a-day! he's dead, he's dead, he's dead!*
We are undone, lady, we are undone!
Alack the day! he's gone, he's kill'd, he's dead!

JULIET
[*Her heart stopping in sudden fear.*]
Can heaven be so envious?

NURSE   Romeo can,
Though heaven cannot. O Romeo, Romeo!
   [*Sitting down on the bench.*]
Who ever would have thought it? Romeo!

JULIET
[*Rushing over to her.*]
What devil art thou, that dost torment me thus?

* *well-a-day:* an expression of sorrow

This torture should be roar'd in dismal hell.
Hath Romeo slain himself?
If he be slain, say ay; or if not, no.
Brief sounds determine of my weal or woe.*

NURSE
[*Rocking back and forth.*]
I saw the wound, I saw it with mine eyes,—
God save the mark!—here on his manly breast.

JULIET
[*Collapsing on the ground beside the old woman.*]
O, break, my heart! poor bankrupt, break at once!
To prison, eyes, ne'er look on liberty!
Vile earth, to earth resign; end motion here;
And thou and Romeo press one heavy bier!
[*That is, let my broken heart be taken to the graveyard with Romeo.*]

NURSE
[*Wailing.*]
O Tybalt, Tybalt, the best friend I had!
O courteous Tybalt! Honest gentleman!†
That ever I should live to see thee dead!

[*Now Juliet lifts her head and stares at the Nurse. Are Romeo and Tybalt, her cousin, both dead?*]

JULIET
What storm is this that blows so contrary?

* *weal or woe:* well-being or misery
† *honest:* honorable

Is Romeo slaught'red, and is Tybalt dead?

NURSE
Tybalt is gone, and Romeo banished;
Romeo that kill'd him, he is banished.

JULIET
[*Up on her knees, trying to get the straight
of the news.*]
O God! did Romeo's hand shed Tybalt's blood?

NURSE
It did, it did; alas the day, it did!

JULIET
[*Pulling herself back violently with a sud-
den sharp feeling of anger against Romeo.*]
O serpent heart, hid with a flow'ring face!
Did ever dragon keep so fair a cave?
        [*She thinks with bitter grief of the con-
        tradictions in Romeo's nature.*]
Beautiful tyrant! fiend angelical!
Dove-feather'd raven! wolvish ravening lamb!
Despised substance of divinest show!
Just opposite to what thou justly seem'st,*
        [*Her voice getting sharper and sharper.*]
A damned saint, an honorable villain!
O nature, what hadst thou to do in hell,
When thou didst bower the spirit of a fiend†
In mortal paradise of such sweet flesh?
        [*She sobs hysterically.*]

* *just:* exact   † *bower:* lodge

NURSE
[*Joining in the weeping.*]
There's no trust,
No faith, no honesty in men; all perjur'd,
All forsworn, all naught, all dissemblers.
Shame come to Romeo!

[*Juliet stops her sobbing suddenly. She can make accusations against Romeo, but she can't stand to have anyone else speak that way.*]

JULIET
                    Blister'd be thy tongue
For such a wish! He was not born to shame.
Upon his brow shame is asham'd to sit;
          [*Away down inside of her she is convinced that Romeo is still good.*]
For 'tis a throne where honor may be crown'd
Sole monarch of the universal earth.
O, what a beast was I to chide at him!

NURSE
[*Amazed.*]
Will you speak well of him that kill'd your cousin?

JULIET
[*Rising.*]
Shall I speak ill of him that is my husband?
          [*Turning from the Nurse and moving toward the right, her voice tender again.*]
Ah, poor my lord, what tongue shall smooth thy
    name,

When I, thy three-hours wife, have mangled it?
       [*She stops. On the verge of tears again.*]
But, wherefore, villain, didst thou kill my cousin?
       [*But then she thinks:*]
That villain cousin would have kill'd my husband.
Back, foolish tears, back to your native spring;
       [*A little note of thankfulness creeping into
       her speech.*]
My husband lives that Tybalt would have slain;
And Tybalt's dead that would have slain my hus-
    band.
       [*Raising her head, her eyes shining.*]
All this is comfort; wherefore weep I then?
       [*But the joy vanishes.*]
Some word there was, worser than Tybalt's death,
That murd'red me; I would forget it fain;
But, O, it presses to my memory
Like damned guilty deeds to sinners' minds:
"Tybalt is dead, and Romeo—banished."
       [*She utters the word "banished" as if it
       were a dagger thrust into her.*]
That "banished," that one word "banished,"
Hath slain ten thousand Tybalts.
"Romeo is banished!"
       [*She moans.*]
There is no end, no limit, measure, bound,
In that word's death; no words can that woe
    sound.*
       [*Turning to the Nurse, her voice hardening.*]

* *sound:* express

Where is my father and my mother, nurse?

NURSE
Weeping and wailing over Tybalt's corse.*
Will you go to them? I will bring you thither.
          [*She rises from the bench.*]

JULIET
Wash they his wounds with tears? Mine shall be
     spent,
When theirs are dry, for Romeo's banishment.
          [*Speaking the word "banishment" nearly
          brings back the sobs.*]
Take up those cords. Poor ropes, you are beguil'd,
Both you and I, for Romeo is exil'd.
He made you for a highway to my bed,
But I, a maid, die maiden-widowed.
Come, cords, come, nurse; I'll to my wedding bed;
And death, not Romeo, take my maidenhead!

NURSE
          [*Going over toward the gate at the right.*]
Hie to your chamber. I'll find Romeo
To comfort you; I wot well where he is.†
Hark ye, your Romeo will be here at night.
I'll to him; he is hid at Laurence' cell.

JULIET
O, find him! Give this ring to my true knight,
          [*Handing her the ring.*]
And bid him come to take his last farewell.

* *corse:* dead body   † *wot:* know

THE VIAL

Romeo and Juliet. act IV, scene 3

JULIET

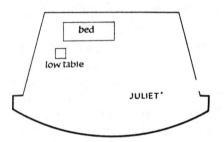

Juliet's bedroom

INTRODUCTION. For his killing of Juliet's cousin, Tybalt, Romeo has been exiled by the Prince. Grief-stricken over his absence and afraid to tell of her secret marriage to Romeo, Juliet is forced to listen to her parents' plans to wed her to her kinsman, Paris. In panic, she has sought Friar Laurence, who has given her a potion which will induce the appearance of death although actually she will be in a deep coma. The plan is for Juliet to appear dead, to be placed in the family vault, and then for Romeo—under cover of darkness —to rescue her from the vault and take her away with

33

him. Juliet, alone in her bedroom now, has said good
night to her mother and the Nurse and is thinking with
terror about what she has to do.

> [*Juliet is standing at the door left through
> which Juliet's mother and the Nurse have
> just gone. Juliet is speaking to herself
> rather than to them.*]

JULIET

Farewell! God knows when we shall meet again.

> [*She takes a step or two toward the center
> of room, turns and shudders.*]

I have a faint cold fear thrills through my veins,
That almost freezes up the heat of life.
I'll call them back again to comfort me.

> [*She runs back to the door and calls.*]

Nurse!

> [*Checking herself.*]

What should she do here?
My dismal scene I needs must act alone.

> [*Juliet walks slowly over to the little table
> by her bed and picks up the small bottle
> containing the sleeping potion given her
> by Friar Laurence.*]

Come, vial.

> [*She looks at it for a long moment.*]

What if this mixture do not work at all?
Shall I be married then tomorrow morning?
No, no; this shall forbid it. Lie thou there.

[*She draws a small dagger from her dress
and puts it on the table within easy reach
of the bed. Now she looks at the vial again.*]
What if it be a poison, which the friar
Subtly hath minist'red to have me dead,*
Lest in this marriage he should be dishonor'd
Because he married me before to Romeo?†
          [*Her voice trembles.*]
I fear it is;
          [*She tries to assure herself.*]
          and yet, methinks, it should not,
For he hath still been tried a holy man.‡
          [*But now she thinks of another horror.*]
How if, when I am laid into the tomb,
I wake before the time that Romeo
Come to redeem me? There's a fearful point!
          [*The bedroom seems to grow small, dark
          and stifling around her.*]
Shall I not then be stifled in the vault,
To whose foul mouth no healthsome air breathes in,
And there die strangled ere my Romeo comes?
Or, if I live, is it not very like
The horrible conceit of death and night,§
          [*Her voice rising in gasping shrillness.*]
Together with the terror of the place,
As in a vault, an ancient receptacle,
Where, for this many hundred years, the bones
Of all my buried ancestors are pack'd;

---

* *minist'red:* fixed   † *before:* already, ahead of time
‡ *he:* Friar Laurence   *still:* ever   *tried:* proved by test to be...
§ *conceit:* idea

[*Shadows of ghosts seem to move around
her. Imagining that she sees the shape of
her recently killed cousin in the right
corner, she retreats to the left.*]

Where bloody Tybalt, yet but green in earth,*
Lies fest'ring in his shroud; where, as they say,
At some hours in the night spirits resort;

[*Now she begins to hear ghostly voices.
She retreats upstage.*]

Alack, alack, is it not like that I,
So early waking, what with loathsome smells,
And shrieks like mandrakes' torn out of the earth,†
That living mortals, hearing them, run mad;

[*Her own voice has almost reached the
shrieking pitch of the ghostly sounds she
thinks she hears.*]

O, if I wake, shall I not be distraught,
Environed with all these hideous fears,
And madly play with my forefathers' joints,
And pluck the mangled Tybalt from his shroud,
And, in this rage, with some great kinsman's bone
As with a club, dash out my desperate brains?

[*She beats her head with her free hand.
Then she seems to see the form of Tybalt
moving toward the door.*]

O, look! methinks I see my cousin's ghost
Seeking out Romeo, that did spit his body

---

* *green in earth:* freshly buried
† *mandrakes':* the root of the mandrake plant was believed to
utter a shriek when pulled up, as if it were alive.

Upon a rapier's point.

> [*Rushing toward the place where she seems to see her cousin.*]

Stay, Tybalt, stay!

> [*Juliet lifts the vial. Slowly and resolutely she walks to the bed, sits down and opens the bottle.*]

Romeo, I come! This do I drink to thee.

> [*She drinks the potion and sinks down on the bed.*]

THE MORE DECEIVED

Hamlet. act III, scene 1

OPHELIA

HAMLET

THE PRESENCES
BEHIND THE SCREEN

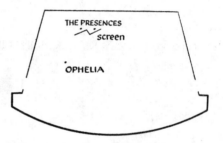

A room in the palace at Elsinore

INTRODUCTION. The King of Denmark has died suddenly, in a mysterious way. His son, young Prince Hamlet, suspects that the man who has become his stepfather and is now wearing the crown is guilty of murder. To gather evidence, Hamlet pretends insanity. The new King fears Hamlet has guessed the truth and begins to question the reality of his madness. Polonius, the Lord Chamberlain and father of Ophelia, thinks it

38

is Hamlet's love for her that is the cause of his distraught condition. To prove this, Polonius arranges a
meeting between the two, which he and the King may
secretly observe from behind a screen. Ophelia is ap-
parently alone as Hamlet enters the room.

> [*Ophelia is standing at the right near the
> screen behind which the King and her fa-
> ther are presumably hiding. Hamlet enters
> quietly at the left. Ophelia tries to be pleas-
> ant, but she is very uncomfortable about
> the role she has to play.*]

> OPHELIA

Good my lord,*
How does your honor for this many a day?

> HAMLET
> [*Sensing at once that there is something
> unnatural in Ophelia's manner.*]

I humbly thank you, well, well, well.

> OPHELIA

My lord, I have remembrances of yours
That I have longed long to re-deliver.
I pray you, now receive them.

> [*She holds out to him perhaps a bracelet
> and a silk handkerchief.*]

> HAMLET
> [*Genuinely hurt.*]   No, no;
> [*Then catching himself.*]

I never gave you aught.

* *Good my lord:* a term of greeting

OPHELIA
My honor'd lord, I know right well you did,
And, with them, words of so sweet breath compos'd
As made the things more rich.
                [*Sighing, a little too obviously.*]
                                        Their perfume lost,
Take these again; for to the noble mind
Rich gifts wax poor when givers prove unkind.
                [*She insists on handing the objects to him.*]
There, my lord.

HAMLET
[*He catches sight of a little movement of
the screen and is immediately suspicious.
His voice hardens.*]
Ha, ha! are you honest?*

OPHELIA
My lord!

HAMLET
Are you fair?

OPHELIA
What means your lordship?
                [*She is a little frightened by his manner.*]

HAMLET
That if you be honest and fair, your honesty
should admit no discourse to your beauty.†

* *honest:* chaste
† *admit no discourse to:* have no communion with

OPHELIA

Could beauty, my lord, have better commerce*
than with honesty?

HAMLET

Ay, truly; for the power of beauty will sooner
transform honesty from what it is to a bawd† than
the force of honesty can translate beauty into his
likeness. This was sometime a paradox, but now
the time gives it proof.

> [*He walks past her to the right, trying to
> speak coldly.*]

I did love you once.

OPHELIA

Indeed, my lord, you made me believe so.

HAMLET

> [*Bursting out. His present bitterness
> springs from his love for her hurt by his
> lack of trust in her.*]

You should not have believ'd me, for virtue cannot so inoculate‡ our old stock but we shall relish§
of it.** I loved you not.

OPHELIA

I was the more deceived.

HAMLET

> [*Almost brutally.*]

Get thee to a nunnery; why wouldst thou be a

---

* *commerce:* intercourse   † *bawd:* prostitute
‡ *inoculate:* engraft   § *relish:* have a trace
** *it:* the old stock. That is, assumed virtue can't change the
basic character of a man.

breeder of sinners? Go thy ways to a nunnery.
> [*Glancing at the screen.*]

Where's your father?

OPHELIA
> [*Hesitatingly.*]

At home, my lord.

HAMLET
> [*Laughing harshly. He shouts the next
> sentence right at the screen.*]

Let the doors be shut upon him, that he may play
the fool nowhere but in's own house.
> [*Starting out right.*]

Farewell!

OPHELIA
> [*Turning left, genuinely distressed.*]

O, help him, you sweet heavens!

HAMLET
> [*Flinging this at her from the doorway.*]

If thou dost marry, I'll give thee this plague for thy
dowry: be thou as chaste as ice, as pure as snow,
thou shalt not escape calumny.* Get thee to a nunnery, go. Farewell!
> [*He turns to the door, then turns back to
> her savagely.*]

Or, if thou wilt needs marry, marry a fool; for wise
men know well enough what monsters you make
of them. To a nunnery, go, and quickly too. Farewell!

* *calumny:* slander

[*He waves her off, as if he expected her to be on her way left.*]

OPHELIA
[*Frightened and deeply hurt.*]
O heavenly powers, restore him!

HAMLET
[*Taking a step toward her.*]
I have heard of your paintings too, well enough. God has given you one face, and you make yourself another. You jig, you amble, and you lisp and nickname God's creatures and make your wantonness your ignorance.* Go to, I'll no more on't; it hath made me mad. I say, we will have no more marriages. Those that are married already all but one† shall live; the rest shall keep as they are. To a nunnery, go.
[*He strides out right. Ophelia, heartsick, stands watching his departure.*]

OPHELIA
O, what a noble mind is here o'erthrown!
The observ'd of all observers, quite, quite down!
[*She turns away suddenly and puts her hands to her eyes.*]
O, woe is me,
T' have seen what I have seen, see what I see!
[*She bursts into tears.*]

---

* *make your wantonness your ignorance:* excuse your affected behavior as ignorance   *Go to:* an expression of impatience
† *all but one:* Hamlet is here referring to his uncle, Claudius.

THE PHANTOM DAGGER

Macbeth. act II, scene 1

MACBETH

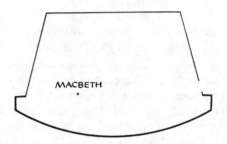

A room in Macbeth's castle

INTRODUCTION. On their way to meet Duncan, King of Scotland, two of his generals, Macbeth and Banquo, are stopped by three witches who prophesy that Macbeth shall first become thane of Cawdor, then King of Scotland, and that Banquo shall beget a line of Kings. They pay little heed at first, but soon after this meeting with the witches Macbeth is made thane of Cawdor by Duncan, and begins to covet the throne. Before Duncan arrives at Macbeth's castle to spend the night Lady Macbeth urges her husband to slay him. Macbeth is now alone in a room in the castle waiting for the moment when he will kill King Duncan.

44

[*Macbeth is standing, as if in a trance, right center.*]

MACBETH
Is this a dagger which I see before me,
The handle toward my hand?
                    [*He puts his hand out for it.*]
                              Come, let me clutch thee.
                    [*But the hand closes on nothing.*]
I have thee not, and yet I see thee still.
Art thou not, fatal vision, sensible*
To feeling as to sight? or art thou but
A dagger of the mind, a false creation,
Proceeding from the heat-oppressed brain?
                    [*After a pause.*]
I see thee yet, in form as palpable
As this which now I draw.
                    [*He pulls out of his belt an actual dagger.*]
Thou marshalls't me the way that I was going,†
And such an instrument I was to use.‡
                    [*He shakes his head and rubs his eyes,
                    trying to clear the image from his sight.*]
Mine eyes are made the fools o' th' other senses,
Or else worth all the rest. I see thee still,§
And on thy blade and dudgeon gouts of blood,**
Which was not so before. There's no such thing.

---

* *sensible:* perceptible
† *Thou marshalls't me:* you point out to me
‡ *instrument:* dagger   § *worth all the rest:* more perceptive
than the other senses   ** *dudgeon:* handle   *gouts:* drops

[He turns from the place where the dagger seems to be and tries to clear his mind of it. The actual dagger is still in his hand.]

It is the bloody business which informs*
Thus to mine eyes. Now o'er the one half-world

[He turns slowly and looks out fearfully to the left.]

Nature seems dead, and wicked dreams abuse†
The curtain'd sleep. Witchcraft celebrates
Pale Hecate's offerings, and wither'd Murder,‡

[The darkness seems to surround him and his eyes shift to the front, then to the right.]

Alarum'd by his sentinel, the wolf,
Whose howl's his watch, thus with his stealthy
  pace,§
With Tarquin's ravishing strides, towards his de-
  sign**
Moves like a ghost.

[With his dagger held out in front of him, Macbeth moves slowly toward the left as if he were being drawn that way.]

             Thou sure and firm set earth,
Hear not my steps, which way they walk, for fear
The very stones prate of my whereabout††

---

* *informs:* speaks † *abuse:* deceive
‡ *Hecate:* goddess of the night and witchcraft
§ *whose howl's his watch:* whose howl tells the listener that it's time for murder *his:* Murder's
** *Tarquin:* a legendary villain *ravishing:* filled with dark emotion *design:* the death he intends to cause
†† *prate:* tell, chatter

And take the present horror from the time,*
Which now suits with it.†

> [*Macbeth squares his shoulders and takes
> a deep breath.*]

Whiles I threat, he lives‡
Words to the heat of deeds too cold breath gives.

> [*Now is the time for action, not words. A
> ghostly bell rings in another part of the
> castle.*]

I go, and it is done; the bell invites me.
Hear it not, Duncan; for it is a knell
That summons thee to heaven or to hell.

> [*Macbeth goes out left.*]

---

* *take the present horror from the time:* take on, or assume,
the horror of the night
† *suits with it:* fits my presence here
‡ *threat:* talk thus about murder   *he:* the King upstairs

THE HOUR FOR MURDER

Macbeth. act II, scene 2

LADY MACBETH

MACBETH

A room in Macbeth's castle

INTRODUCTION. This is the night for the murder of King Duncan. Lady Macbeth has drugged the King's attendants so that her husband may kill him quietly, then laid the weapons in their hands to point the suspicion at them. She is now in a room, awaiting Macbeth's return.

48

[*Lady Macbeth has been pacing the floor, and now stands left center.*]

LADY MACBETH

That which hath made them drunk hath made me bold;*
What hath quench'd them hath given me fire. Hark!
    [*She hears something. Then she relaxes a little.*]
    Peace!
It was the owl that shriek'd, the fatal bellman†
Which gives the stern'st good night. He is about it.‡
The doors are open, and the surfeited grooms§
Do mock their charge with snores. I have drugg'd their possets,**
That death and nature do contend about them††
Whether they live or die.

[*Macbeth enters left, carrying two daggers, then turns abruptly as if he heard someone.*]

MACBETH

Who's there? What, ho!

---

* *that:* the wine   † *bellman:* the night watchman who customarily visited prisoners before their execution
‡ *He is about it:* Macbeth, as the executioner
§ *surfeited:* drunken   *grooms:* King's body servants
** *mock their charge with snores:* make a mockery of their responsibility by snoring   *possets:* drink made of wine and hot milk
†† *contend about them whether they:* have a contest in making them appear to

[*Lady Macbeth continues to speak her own thoughts.*]

LADY MACBETH

Alack, I am afraid they have awak'd,*
And 'tis not done.†

[*Still not seeing her husband.*]

Th' attempt and not the deed
Confounds us. Hark!‡

[*Again she thinks she hears some stirring upstairs. How could Macbeth have bungled the killing?*]

I laid their daggers ready;
He could not miss 'em. Had he not resembled§
My father as he slept, I had done 't.

[*Now she suddenly notices Macbeth with his bloody hands.*]

My husband!

MACBETH

[*Turning slowly with his voice full of quiet horror.*]

I have done the deed. Didst thou not hear a noise?

LADY MACBETH

I heard the owl scream and the crickets cry.
Did not you speak?

MACBETH

When?

---

* *they:* the King's servants
† *'tis not done:* the murder hasn't been effected (by Macbeth)
‡ *confounds:* will destroy   § *Had he:* had the King

LADY MACBETH
Now.

MACBETH
As I descended?

LADY MACBETH
Ay.

MACBETH
[*Again, he turns his head to the left, listening.*]
Hark!
[*Whispering.*]
Who lies i' th' second chamber?

LADY MACBETH
Donalbain.

MACBETH
[*Looking at his blood-stained hands holding the daggers.*]
This is a sorry sight.

LADY MACBETH
[*Reproving him to calm herself as well as her husband.*]
A foolish thought, to say a sorry sight.

MACBETH
[*Looking back to where he has been.*]
There's one did laugh in 's sleep, and one cried,
   "Murder!"
That they did wake each other. I stood and heard
   them;
But they did say their prayers, and address'd them
Again to sleep.

LADY MACBETH
There are two lodg'd together.

[*Macbeth recreates the scene in his mind, slowly, quietly imitating the sound of the innocent servants' voices.*]

MACBETH
One cried, "God bless us!" and "Amen" the other,
As they had seen me with these hangman's hands,*
List'ning their fear. I could not say "Amen"
When they did say, "God bless us!"

LADY MACBETH
[*Trying to rally him out of his fear.*]
Consider it not so deeply.

MACBETH
[*Turning to his wife beseechingly, almost in tears.*]
But wherefore could not I pronounce "Amen"?
I had most need of blessing, and "Amen"
Stuck in my throat.

LADY MACBETH
These deeds must not be thought
After these ways; so, it will make us mad.†

MACBETH
[*Still in a black daze with his hands held out in front of him.*]
Methought I heard a voice cry, "Sleep no more!

---

* *hangman's hands:* In Shakespeare's time the hangman's hands were bloody because in an execution for treason he tore out the victim's entrails.
† *after these ways; so, it:* in this way, or they ...

Macbeth does murder sleep"—the innocent sleep,
Sleep that knits up the ravell'd sleave of care,*
The death of each day's life, sore labor's bath,
Balm of hurt minds, great nature's second course,
Chief nourisher in life's feast.
> [*How he longs to be able to go to sleep
> and forget his awful deed!*]

LADY MACBETH

What do you mean?

MACBETH

Still it cried, "Sleep no more!" to all the house;
"Glamis hath murder'd sleep, and therefore Caw-
 dor†
Shall sleep no more; Macbeth shall sleep no more."

LADY MACBETH
> [*Beginning to get frightened and angry at
> her husband.*]

Who was it that thus cried? Why, worthy thane,
You do unbend your noble strength, to think
So brainsickly of things. Go get some water,
And wash this filthy witness from your hand.‡
> [*Macbeth still has the daggers in his hands.*]

Why did you bring these daggers from the place?
They must lie there. Go carry them; and smear
The sleepy grooms with blood.

---

* *ravell'd sleave:* tangled skein
† *Glamis:* Macbeth is thane of Glamis   *Cawdor:* The witches
told Macbeth that he would become thane of Cawdor.
‡ *this filthy witness:* the blood

MACBETH
[*In a low but emphatic voice.*]
                              I'll go no more.
I am afraid to think what I have done;
Look on't again I dare not.

LADY MACBETH   Infirm of purpose!
Give me the daggers.
          [*She seizes them from him.*]
                    The sleeping and the dead
Are but as pictures; 'tis the eye of childhood
That fears a painted devil. If he do bleed,*
I'll gild the faces of the grooms withal;†
For it must seem their guilt.
          [*Lady Macbeth goes out left. There is a
          distant sound of knocking.*]

MACBETH   Whence is that knocking?
How is't with me, when every noise appalls me?‡
          [*Looking at his blood-covered hands again,
          almost as if they didn't belong to him.*]
What hands are here? Ha! they pluck out mine
     eyes.
Will all great Neptune's ocean wash this blood§
Clean from my hand? No, this my hand will rather
The multitudinous seas incarnadine,**
Making the green one red.
          [*He stands transfixed.*]

* *he:* the King   † *withal:* with it (the blood)
‡ *appalls me:* frightens me, makes me pale
§ *Neptune:* god of the sea   ** *incarnadine:* turn blood-red

DARK FORMS IN THE MIND

Macbeth. act III, scene 2

LADY MACBETH

MACBETH

A room in Macbeth's castle

INTRODUCTION. King Duncan is dead and Macbeth has succeeded him to the throne. Banquo suspects Macbeth of the murder, and Macbeth in turn fears Banquo because of the witches' prophecy that his descendents, not Macbeth's, will hold the kingship. Macbeth arranges for Banquo to be slain. Lady Macbeth has sent a message to Macbeth requesting him to come to her room so she can talk with him. She awaits him there now.

55

LADY MACBETH

Nought's had, all's spent,
Where our desire is got without content.*
'Tis safer to be that which we destroy
Than by destruction dwell in doubtful joy.

> [*Lady Macbeth means it would be better
> to be the murdered person now at rest,
> than the live murderer worrying himself
> sick over what he has done. She is think-
> ing now both of herself and of Macbeth.
> He enters and she turns to him quietly.*]

How now, my lord! why do you keep alone,†
Of sorriest fancies your companions making,‡
Using those thoughts which should indeed have
   died§
With them they think on? Things without all
   remedy
Should be without regard; what's done is done.

> [*She is trying to brace him up. The murder
> has been done, now forget it!*]

MACBETH
[*Shuddering.*]

We have scotch'd the snake, not kill'd it;**
She'll close and be herself, whilst our poor malice††
Remains in danger of her former tooth.

---

* *content:* contentment
† *How now, my lord:* a term of greeting   *keep:* keep yourself
‡ *of sorriest fancies:* making your companions the darkest kind
of mental images   § *using:* keeping company with
** *scotched:* gashed   †† *close:* reunite

> [*Macbeth means simply that though we have killed one man—the King—we are not out of danger, for there are alive many who may suspect us.*]

But let the frame of things disjoint, both the worlds
  suffer,*
Ere we will eat our meal in fear and sleep
In the affliction of these terrible dreams
That shake us nightly.

> [*We shall have to let suspicions of our awful deed die somehow before we can eat our meals and sleep at night, even with fear still haunting us.*]

Duncan is in his grave;

> [*He almost envies him.*]

After life's fitful fever he sleeps well.
Treason has done his worst; nor steel, nor poison,†
Malice domestic, foreign levy, nothing,
Can touch him further.

> [*Lady Macbeth tries now to rouse her husband out of his dark mood by talking straight to him. Perhaps she shakes him, smiling at him.*]

LADY MACBETH
              Come on,
Gentle my lord, sleek o'er your rugged looks;‡

---

* *both the worlds:* the two parts of the snake (symbolizing gossip, suspicion)   *suffer:* suffer death
† *steel:* referring to daggers or swords
‡ *Gentle my lord:* my gentlemanly lord   *sleek:* smooth

Be bright and jovial among your guests tonight.
> [*Remember you have guests, and you musn't let them suspect anything.*]

MACBETH
> [*With a long breath, lifting his head, trying to be resolute.*]

So shall I, love; and so, I pray, be you.
Let your remembrance apply to Banquo;
> [*Keep talking about Banquo.*]

Present him eminence both with eye and tongue.*
> [*He drops his head as fear grips him again.*]

Unsafe the while that we
Must lave our honors in these flattering streams,†
And make our faces vizards to our hearts,‡
Disguising what they are.
> [*Macbeth is saying in effect that pretending will be difficult. We shall talk about our love for Banquo, knowing at the same time that we have wanted his death.*]

LADY MACBETH

        You must leave this.
> [*Stop thinking these thoughts!*]

MACBETH
> [*Bursting out.*]

O, full of scorpions is my mind, dear wife!
Thou know'st that Banquo, and his Fleance lives.§

---

* *eminence:* special favor   † *lave:* bathe   ‡ *vizards:* masks
§ *Fleance:* Banquo's son

LADY MACBETH
But in them nature's copy's not eterne.
> [*Remember that their lease—copy—on
> life is not eternal. Lady Macbeth is hint-
> ing that another murder might be com-
> mitted.*]

MACBETH
There's comfort yet; they are assailable.*
Then be thou jocund;†
> [*Macbeth laughs wildly for a moment,
> then stops and drops his voice to a whisper.*]
>   ere the bat hath flown
His cloister'd flight, ere to black Hecate's sum-
    mons‡
The shard-borne beetle with his drowsy hums§
Hath rung night's yawning peal, there shall be done
A deed of dreadful note.

LADY MACBETH
> [*Pretending that she hasn't put the idea of
> the new murder into his mind.*]
>   What's to be done?

MACBETH
> [*With a forced smile.*]
Be innocent of the knowledge, dearest chuck,**
Till thou applaud the deed. Come, seeling night,††

---

* *assailable:* vulnerable   † *jocund:* merry
‡ *cloistered:* hidden   *Hecate:* the goddess of night and witchcraft   § *shard-borne:* borne on hard wings
** *chuck:* term of endearment   †† *seeling:* blinding

Scarf up the tender eye of pitiful day,*
And with thy bloody and invisible hand
Cancel and tear to pieces that great bond†
Which keeps me pale! Light thickens, and the crow
       [*Macbeth is getting caught up in the black
       spirit of the night.*]
Makes wing to the rooky wood;‡
Good things of day begin to droop and drowse,
Whiles night's black agents to their preys do
  rouse.§
Thou marvell'st at my words, but hold thee still;
       [*He is telling Lady Macbeth not to be so
       surprised by his change of manner. He can
       be just as hard and cunning as she!*]
Things bad begun make strong themselves by ill.
       [*Since we've made ourselves villains we
       might as well be villains all the way!*]
So prithee go with me.
       [*He leads her roughly out the door, right.*]

---

* *scarf up:* put a scarf over, blindfold   † *bond:* Banquo's life
‡ *rooky:* haunted by rooks   § *their preys do rouse:* rouse
themselves to prey on other creatures

THE SLEEPWALKER

Macbeth. act V, scene 1

LADY MACBETH

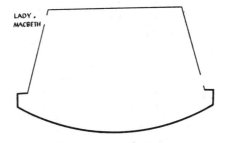

A hallway in Macbeth's castle

INTRODUCTION. Banquo has been murdered, but his son, Fleance, has escaped. Macbeth has had a second meeting with the witches and, after hearing their predictions, has caused the death of the wife and children of a friend of his. Lady Macbeth has become worried by the passing events and has begun to walk in her sleep. It is night in a hallway of the castle.

[*Lady Macbeth enters slowly up right, as in a trance, with a candle in her hand. After she has taken a few steps she stops and looks at her free hand. She speaks with horror.*]

LADY MACBETH

Yet here's a spot. Out, damned spot! out, I say!
[*Suddenly her voice becomes thin and high. She speaks without meaning.*]
One: two: why, then 'tis time to do't.
[*Looking around her at the shadows, shuddering.*]
Hell is murky!
[*With a voice suddenly firm, as if she were addressing her husband.*]
Fie, my lord, fie! a soldier, and afeard? What need we fear who knows it, when none can call our pow'r to account?
[*Whimpering like a little girl who has cut her finger.*]
Yet who would have thought the old man to have had so much blood in him?
[*Now matter of fact as she moves across the stage.*]
The thane of Fife had a wife; where is she now?
[*Stopping convulsively as she looks at her hands again.*]
What, will these hands ne'er be clean?

[*To her husband again.*]
No more o' that, my lord, no more o' that; you mar all* with this starting.†

[*Almost crying with the pain of her horror.*]
Here's the smell of the blood still; all the perfumes of Arabia will not sweeten this little hand. Oh, oh, oh!

[*Firmly once more. Her mind has jumped again.*]
Wash your hands, put on your nightgown; look not so pale.

[*To her imaginary husband, as if he were a child.*]
I tell you yet again, Banquo's buried; he cannot come out on's grave. To bed, to bed! There's knocking at the gate. Come, come, come, come, give me your hand. What's done cannot be undone. To bed, to bed, to bed!

[*Her voice trails off into the distance as she goes out the passageway down left.*]

---

* *mar all:* spoil everything
† *starting:* sudden movement (in fear)

PORTIA'S WARNING

Julius Caesar. act II, scene 1

BRUTUS

PORTIA

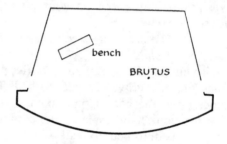

The garden of Brutus' home

INTRODUCTION. Julius Caesar, the dictator of Rome, has returned to the capital victorious. He has conquered Pompey, his former rival, and stands now at the height of his power. Cassius, Casca, Marcus Brutus, and others, fear that Caesar has gained too much power and that he will use it to crown himself king. A conspiracy is formed to murder Caesar and the plotters ask Brutus to join them, but he hesitates, weighing his friendship for Caesar against Caesar's threat to the state. Finally, reluctantly he is persuaded to believe that Caesar is a tyrant and must be assassi-

64

nated. It is early morning. The conspirators have just left and Brutus is alone in his garden pondering over the decision he has made.

> [*Brutus is standing at the left, looking thoughtfully off to the left.*]

> PORTIA
> [*Entering from the right.*]

Brutus, my lord!

> BRUTUS
> [*Turning and looking at her with haggard eyes.*]

Portia, what mean you? Wherefore rise you now?
> [*Going to her and putting his arm around her solicitously.*]

It is not for your health thus to commit
Your weak condition to the raw cold morning.

> PORTIA

Nor for yours neither. You've ungently, Brutus,*
Stole from my bed; and yesternight at supper
You suddenly arose and walk'd about,
Musing and sighing, with your arms across;†
And when I ask'd you what the matter was,
You star'd upon me with ungentle looks.
I urg'd you further; then you scratch'd your head
And too impatiently stamp'd with your foot.
Yet I insisted; yet you answer'd not,
But with an angry wafture of your hand‡

---

* *ungently:* unkindly   † *across:* across your chest
‡ *wafture:* waving

Gave sign for me to leave you. So I did,
Fearing to strengthen that impatience
Which seem'd too much enkindled, and withal*
Hoping it was but an effect of humor,†
Which sometime hath his hour with every man.
              [*Almost in tears.*]
It will not let you eat, nor talk, nor sleep,
And could it work so much upon your shape‡
As it hath much prevail'd on your condition,§
I should not know you, Brutus. Dear my lord,
Make me acquainted with your cause of grief.
              [*She turns her face to his appealingly.*]

        BRUTUS
        [*Dropping his eyes because he doesn't
        wish to look at her.*]
I am not well in health, and that is all.

        PORTIA
        [*Still appealingly.*]
Brutus is wise, and were he not in health,
He would embrace the means to come by it.**

        [*Brutus tries to lead Portia gently back to
        the right toward the house.*]

        BRUTUS
Why, so I do. Good Portia, go to bed.

* *withal:* at the same time   † *humor:* melancholy disposition
‡ *shape:* appearance   § *condition:* nature
** *embrace the means:* find a way

PORTIA
[*Refusing to be led and turning to Brutus.*]
What, is Brutus sick,
And will he steal out of his wholesome bed
To dare the vile contagion of the night,
And tempt the rheumy and unpurged air*
To add unto his sickness? No, my Brutus;
You have some sick offence within your mind,
Which, by the right and virtue of my place,
I ought to know of; and upon my knees
    [*Getting down on her knees.*]
I charm you, by my once commended beauty,†
By all your vows of love, and that great vow
Which did incorporate and make us one,
That you unfold to me, yourself, your half,
Why you are heavy, and what men tonight‡
Have had resort to you; for here have been§
Some six or seven, who did hide their faces
Even from darkness.

    [*Brutus lifts Portia.*]

BRUTUS   Kneel not, gentle Portia.

PORTIA
I should not need, if you were gentle Brutus.**
Dwell I but in the suburbs††
Of your good pleasure? If it be no more,
    [*Moving away from him toward the left.*]

---

* *rheumy:* dank   *unpurged:* not yet purified by the sun
† *charm:* conjure   ‡ *heavy:* depressed
§ *resort to you:* come to see you   ** *I should not need:* I
should not have to kneel   †† *suburbs:* outskirts

Portia is Brutus' harlot, not his wife.

BRUTUS
[*Following her.*]
You are my true and honorable wife,
As dear to me as are the ruddy drops
That visit my sad heart.

PORTIA
[*Turning toward him half angrily.*]
If this were true, then should I know this secret.
Tell me your counsels, I will not disclose 'em.*
I have made strong proof of my constancy,†
Giving myself a voluntary wound
Here, in the thigh; can I bear that with patience,
And not my husband's secrets?

BRUTUS
[*Going over to her and impulsively putting an arm around her.*]
　　　　　　　　　　O ye gods!
Render me worthy of this noble wife!
[*He hears the sound of knocking off left. His face hardens.*]
Hark, hark! one knocks. Portia, go in awhile,
And by and by thy bosom shall partake
The secrets of my heart.
[*He pushes her gently but firmly toward the right.*]
Leave me with haste.
[*Portia goes out and Brutus turns left.*]

---

* *counsels:* secrets
† *constancy:* steady good sense and faithful loyalty

CALPURNIA'S WARNING

Julius Caesar. act II, scene 2

CAESAR

SERVANT

CALPURNIA

DECIUS

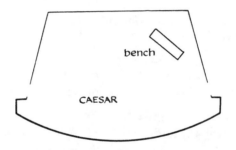

A room in Caesar's home

INTRODUCTION. Brutus has joined the conspirators plotting the death of Caesar. Brutus' heart is heavy at the thought of the task which lies before him. Promising his wife, Portia, to confide in her later, he leaves to set the plan in motion. Unaware of the plot to murder him, Caesar too has spent a restless night, and in his rooms he paces the floor.

69

[*Caesar paces from right to left, left to right, pauses thoughtfully, then paces back to the left. He looks upward toward the front as if he were gazing through a window.*]

CAESAR

Nor heaven nor earth have been at peace tonight.
Thrice hath Calpurnia in her sleep cried out,
"Help! ho! they murder Caesar!"
[*He turns toward the right and calls.*]
Who's within?

SERVANT
[*Entering from the right.*]
My lord?

CAESAR

Go bid the priests do present sacrifice*
And bring me their opinions of success.†

SERVANT

I will, my lord.
[*He goes out the way he came in. Caesar takes a step to the left, then turns as if he were going to follow the servant, when Calpurnia enters quietly from the left. Caesar stops when he hears his wife's voice.*]

CALPURNIA

What mean you, Caesar? Think you to walk forth?

---

* *present:* immediate   † *success:* the outcome of the coming events

You shall not stir out of your house today.

CAESAR
[*Resolutely.*]
Caesar shall forth. The things that threaten'd me
Ne'er look'd but on my back; when they shall see*
The face of Caesar, they are vanished.

CALPURNIA
Caesar, I never stood on ceremonies,†
Yet now they fright me. There is one within,‡
[*Calpurnia looks toward the left.*]
Besides the things that we have heard and seen,
Recounts most horrid sights seen by the watch.
[*She shivers as she recounts the awful
happenings.*]
A lioness hath whelped in the streets,
And graves have yawn'd and yielded up their dead;
Fierce fiery warriors fought upon the clouds
In ranks and squadrons and right form of war,§
Which drizzl'd blood upon the Capitol;
[*Sinking on the bench and putting her
face in her hands.*]
The noise of battle hurtled in the air,
Horses did neigh, and dying men did groan,
And ghosts did shriek and squeal about the streets.
[*Lifting her face toward her husband.*]
O Caesar! these things are beyond all use,**
And I do fear them.

* *but:* except   † *stood on ceremonies:* gave serious thought to
omens   ‡ *one within:* a person inside the house
§ *right:* regular   ** *use:* custom

CAESAR
[*Coming over and sitting beside her.*]
                What can be avoided
Whose end is purpos'd by the mighty gods?
        [*After a moment, straightening up.*]
Yet Ceasar shall go forth; for these predictions
Are to the world in general as to Caesar.*

CALPURNIA
[*Shivering.*]
When beggers die there are no comets seen.
The heavens themselves blaze forth the death of
    princes.

CAESAR
[*Putting his arm around her and letting
her put her head on his shoulder.*]
Cowards die many times before their deaths;
The valiant never taste of death but once.
Of all the wonders that I yet have heard,
It seems to me most strange that men should fear,
Seeing that death, a necessary end,
Will come when it will come.
        [*The Servant re-enters right.*]
                        What say the augurers?

SERVANT
They would not have you to stir forth today.
Plucking the entrails of an offering forth,
They could not find a heart within the beast.

* *are to:* apply as much to

CAESAR
[*Rising and speaking slowly.*]
The gods do this in shame of cowardice;
Caesar should be a beast without a heart,
If he should stay at home today for fear.
No, Caesar shall not.*

CALPURNIA
[*Also rising.*]
            Alas, my lord,
Your wisdom is consum'd in confidence.
[*Appealingly.*]
Do not go forth today; call it my fear
That keeps you in the house, and not your own.
[*Taking Caesar's arm, trying to persuade
him.*]
We'll send Mark Antony to the Senate House,
And he shall say you are not well today.
[*Sinking to her knees.*]
Let me, upon my knee, prevail in this.
[*Caesar looks down at his wife, then at the
Servant. He takes a deep breath before he
speaks, somewhat reluctantly.*]

CAESAR
Mark Antony shall say I am not well;
And, for thy humor, I will stay at home.†
[*He is gently raising Calpurnia when De-
cius, one of the conspirators, enters right.*]
Here's Decius Brutus, he shall tell them so.

---

* *shall not:* shall not stay at home   † *humor:* whim

DECIUS

Caesar, all hail! Good morrow, worthy Caesar;
I come to fetch you to the Senate House.

CAESAR
[*Stepping over center toward him.*]
And you are come in very happy time
To bear my greetings to the Senators
And tell them that I will not come today
Cannot, is false, and that I dare not, falser;
I will not come today. Tell them so, Decius.

CALPURNIA

Say he is sick.

CAESAR
[*Swinging toward his wife.*]
                    Shall Caesar send a lie?
Have I in conquest stretch'd mine arm so far,
To be afeard to tell graybeards the truth?
          [*Turning back to Decius and speaking
          quietly.*]
Decius, go tell them Caesar will not come.

DECIUS
[*In a tone of assumed surprise.*]
Most mighty Caesar, let me know some cause,
Lest I be laugh'd at when I tell them so.

CAESAR
[*Firmly.*]
The cause is in my will; I will not come;
That is enough to satisfy the Senate.

[*Now he walks over to Decius and speaks
confidentially.*]
But for your private satisfaction,
Because I love you, I will let you know:
Calpurnia here, my wife, stays me at home.*
She dreamt tonight she saw my statue,
[*Laughing gently as if he were indulging his
wife's superstitious fancies, not his own.*]
Which, like a fountain with an hundred spouts,
Did run pure blood; and many lusty Romans
Came smiling and did bathe their hands in it;
And these does she apply for warnings and portents
And evils imminent, and on her knee
Hath begg'd that I will stay at home today.

DECIUS
[*With assumed indignation.*]
This dream is all amiss interpreted;
It was a vision fair and fortunate.
Your statue spouting blood in many pipes,
In which so many smiling Romans bath'd,
Signifies that from you great Rome shall suck
Reviving blood, and that great men shall press
For tinctures, stains, relics, and cognizance.†
This by Calpurnia's dream is signified.
[*Calpurnia sinks onto the bench, knowing
she is defeated. Caesar looks at his wife,
then back at Decius.*]

CAESAR
And this way have you well expounded it.

* *stays:* detains   † *cognizance:* tokens

DECIUS
I have, when you have heard what I can say;
And know it now. The Senate have concluded
To give this day a crown to mighty Caesar.
If you shall send them word you will not come,
Their minds may change. Besides, it were a mock
Apt to be render'd, for some one to say,*
"Break up the Senate till another time,
          [*With a note of sarcasm.*]
When Caesar's wife shall meet with better dreams."
If Caesar hide himself, shall they not whisper,
"Lo, Caesar is afraid"?
Pardon me, Caesar; for my dear dear love
          [*He drops his voice to an apologetic tone.*]
To your proceeding bids me tell you this;†
And reason to my love is liable.‡

CAESAR
[*Taking a deep breath and looking at De-
cius. He is afraid now to say no. So he
turns to his wife, putting on an attitude of
bravery which he does not feel.*]
How foolish do your fears seem now, Calpurnia!
I am ashamed I did yield to them.
          [*Turning to the Servant at the door.*]
Give me my robe, for I will go.

          [*Caesar, Decius and the Servant go out
          right, leaving the shocked Calpurnia sit-
          ting on the bench.*]

_____
* *apt:* likely   † *proceeding:* career   ‡ *liable:* subservient

THE STORM

King Lear. act III, scene 2

KING LEAR

THE FOOL

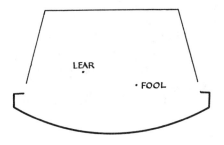

An open heath

INTRODUCTION. Advanced in years, King Lear has divided his kingdom of Britain between two of his three daughters. The third he has banished because, unlike her two sisters, she will not debase herself nor her true regard for her father by making insincere protestations of love for him. Lear goes first to live with his eldest daughter, Goneril, who makes life so unpleasant for him that he is compelled to leave. Journeying to the house of his second daughter, Regan, who is in conspiracy with Goneril, he finds that Regan

77

will allow him to enter her home only under the most demanding of conditions. Disillusioned and angry at his wicked daughters, Lear heads out onto a stormy heath with only his Fool for company.

> [*Lear is bracing himself against the fury of the wind and rain and trying to outshout them and the thunder. The frightened figure of the poor little Fool is crouched in a heap near him.*]

LEAR

Blow, winds, and crack your cheeks! Rage! Blow!
You cataracts and hurricanoes, spout
Till you have drench'd our steeples, drown'd the
    cocks!*

> [*There is a flash of blinding light and a roar of thunder.*]

You sulph'rous and thought-executing fires,
Vaunt-couriers of oak-cleaving thunderbolts,†
Singe my white head! And thou, all-shaking thun-
    der,

> [*He shakes his two fists at it.*]

Strike flat the thick rotundity o' th' world!

> [*The thunder roars again.*]

Crack nature's moulds, all germens spill at once‡
That makes ingrateful man!
Rumble thy bellyful! Spit, fire! Spout, rain!
Nor rain, wind, thunder, fire are my daughters.

---

* *cocks:* weather cocks
† *vaunt-couriers:* forerunners   ‡ *germens:* germs, seeds

[*He cries unashamedly in self-pity.*]
I tax not you, you elements, with unkindness;
I never gave you kingdom, call'd you children;
You owe me no subscription.*
        [*Shouting at the storm again as if challeng-*
        ing it to do its worst.]
                    Then let fall
Your horrible pleasure.
        [*His rain-drenched face is flooded with*
        tears.]
                 Here I stand your slave,
A poor, infirm, weak, and despis'd old man;
        [*Raising his voice again.*]
But yet I call you servile ministers,
That will with two pernicious daughters join
Your high-engender'd battles 'gainst a head†
So old and white as this.

        [NOTE TO THE ACTOR: *In playing this scene*
it will not be so necessary actually to shout as to raise
the pitch of your voice as if you were shouting—push-
ing your words slowly and strongly against the roaring
of the storm.]

* *subscription:* allegiance
† *high-engendered:* produced in the sky

THE FALL

King Lear. act IV, scene 6

EDGAR

GLOUCESTER

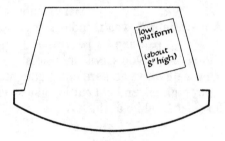

A field near Dover

INTRODUCTION. King Lear's friend, the Earl of Gloucester, has been caught in the confusion resulting from the division of the kingdom. He loses control of his house to Lear's daughter Regan, and she forbids the Earl to aid her father. Gloucester ignores her orders and helps Lear to escape to Dover. As punishment Gloucester's illegitimate son, Edmund, and Regan's husband, Cornwall, blind the Earl and he is set forth on the heath to wander. Now Gloucester has been found by his good son, Edgar, against whom he

80

was turned by what the villainous Edmund had said about him. Gloucester asks to be led to a high cliff, at Dover. But Edgar suspects what the old man has in mind, and takes him into an open field, instead.

[*Edgar leads in the blind Gloucester slowly from the left.*]

GLOUCESTER
[*Stopping for a moment to get his breath.*]
When shall I come to th' top of that same hill?

EDGAR
[*Speaking in a slightly assumed tone of voice so Gloucester won't recognize him.*]
You do climb up it now; look, how we labor.
[*He guides the old man up the downstage edge of the low platform.*]

GLOUCESTER
Methinks the ground is even.

EDGAR   Horrible steep.
[*Turning the old man around to face toward the right.*]
Hark, do you hear the sea?

GLOUCESTER   No truly.

EDGAR
Why, then, your other senses grow imperfect
By your eyes' anguish.

GLOUCESTER
[*Sighing.*]
　　　　　So may it be, indeed.
[*He turns his face toward Edgar.*]
Methinks thy voice is alter'd, and thou speak'st
In better phrase and matter than thou didst.

EDGAR
You're much deceiv'd. In nothing am I chang'd
But in my garments.

GLOUCESTER
　　　　Methinks you're better spoken.*
[*Edgar leads the old man around to the
right edge of the platform.*]

EDGAR
Come on, sir, here's the place; stand still. How
　fearful
And dizzy 'tis, to cast one's eyes so low!
[*He turns his face downward, hoping that
Gloucester will think that he's actually
looking over the edge of a high cliff.*]
The crows and choughs that wing the midway air†
Show scarce so gross as beetles.
[*After a moment as if he were looking at
new details.*]
　　　　　　　Half way down
Hangs one that gathers samphire, dreadful trade!‡
Methinks he seems no bigger than his head.

---

* *you're better spoken:* you speak more like a gentleman
† *choughs:* jackdaws　‡ *samphire:* a seacoast plant

The fishermen that walk upon the beach
Appear like mice; and yond tall anchoring bark,
Diminish'd to her cock; her cock, a buoy*
Almost too small for sight. The murmuring surge,
That on th' unnumb'red idle pebbles chafes,
Cannot be heard so high.
                [*Turning around.*]
                        I'll look no more,
Lest my brain turn, and the deficient sight†
Topple down headlong.

        GLOUCESTER
                  Set me where you stand.
        EDGAR
        [*Pulling him gently to the right edge of the
        platform.*]
Give me your hand; you are now within a foot
Of th' extreme verge. For all beneath the moon
Would I not leap upright.

        GLOUCESTER
                  Let go my hand.
        [*He pulls a purse from his belt.*]
Here, friend, 's another purse; in it a jewel
Well worth a poor man's taking. Fairies and gods
Prosper it with thee! Go thou further off;
        [*Edgar moves a little to the left and
        watches his father.*]
Bid me farewell, and let me hear thee going.

* *cock:* cockboat
† *deficient sight topple:* deficient sight makes me topple

EDGAR
[*Making his voice seem to come from a
greater distance.*]
Now fare ye well, good sir.

GLOUCESTER
                    With all my heart.

EDGAR
Why I do trifle thus with his despair
[*This inward remark is uttered in a half
whisper, to himself, not to Gloucester.*]
Is done to cure it.

GLOUCESTER
[*Kneeling in a quiet last prayer.*]
                    O you mighty gods!
This world I do renounce, and in your sights
Shake patiently my great affliction off.
If I could bear it longer, and not fall
To quarrel with your great opposeless wills,
My snuff and loathed part of nature should*
Burn itself out. If Edgar live, O bless him!
[*He rises, turns his face toward his young
companion and raises his voice a little.*]
Now, fellow, fare thee well.
[*He reaches for the edge with his foot and
topples over, falling in a heap on the floor.
Edgar comes to the edge of the platform
and looks down at the old man. He speaks
to himself.*]

* *snuff:* burnt wick, useless remnant

EDGAR
Gone, sir; farewell!
        [*To himself, in a half whisper.*]
—And yet I know not how conceit may rob*
The treasury of life, when life itself
Yields to the theft. Had he been where he thought,
By this had thought been past.
        [*He steps down and examines the crum-
        pled body.*]
                                Alive or dead?—
        [*He touches his father, assuming now the
        natural voice of Edgar.*]
Ho, you sir! friend! Hear you, sir! speak!
        [*To himself.*]
Thus might he pass indeed; yet he revives.†
        [*Out loud, again.*]
What are you, sir?‡

        GLOUCESTER
        [*Whispering.*]
                Away, and let me die.

        EDGAR
Hadst thou been aught but gossamer, feathers,
        air,§
So many fathom down precipitating,
Thou 'dst shiver'd like an egg: but thou dost
        breathe;**

* *conceit:* imagination   † *might he pass indeed:* he might
actually have died through imagining a long fall down the cliff
‡ *what:* how   § *aught but:* anything except   ** *shiver'd*
shattered

Hast heavy substance, bleed'st not, speak'st, art
   sound.
> [*Edgar speaks as if he is amazed that the
> old man could have fallen so far and re-
> mained alive!*]

Ten masts at each make not the altitude*
Which thou hast perpendicularly fell.
Thy life's a miracle. Speak yet again.

GLOUCESTER
> [*Raising himself gingerly.*]

But have I fall'n, or no?

EDGAR

From the dread summit of this chalky bourn.†
Look up a-height; the shrill-gorg'd lark so far
Cannot be seen or heard. Do but look up.

GLOUCESTER

Alack, I have no eyes.
> [*He is on the verge of tears.*]

Is wretchedness depriv'd that benefit,
To end itself by death? 'Twas yet some comfort,
When misery could beguile the tyrant's rage,
And frustrate his proud will.
> [*That is, Gloucester felt a certain kind of
> satisfaction when he believed he could
> cheat a tyrant out of his persecution by
> putting an end to his own life. But now he
> sees no escape.*]

---

* *at each:* **end to end**   † *bourn:* boundary, cliff

EDGAR
                    Give me your arm.
[*Lifting him up.*]
Up: so. How is't? Feel you your legs? You stand.

GLOUCESTER
Too well, too well.
        [*He had not wanted to stay alive.*]

EDGAR
                This is above all strangeness.
Upon the crown o' th' cliff, what thing was that
Which parted from you?

GLOUCESTER
            A poor unfortunate beggar.

EDGAR
As I stood here below, methought his eyes
Were two full moons; he had a thousand noses,
Horns whelk'd and waved like the enraged sea.*
It was some fiend; therefore, thou happy father,
Think that the clearest gods, who make them
    honors
Of men's impossibilities, have preserv'd thee.
            [*Edgar is trying to make the old man be-
            lieve that what made him jump was the
            power of a devil pretending to be a young
            human companion. But good Providence
            preserved him!*]

* *whelk'd:* twisted

GLOUCESTER
[*Thoughtfully.*]
I do remember now. Henceforth I'll bear
Affliction till it do cry out itself,
"Enough, enough," and die. That thing you
    speak of,
I took it for a man; often 't would say,
"The fiend, the fiend!" He led me to that place.

EDGAR
Bear free and patient thoughts.
        [*Cheerfully but tenderly he leads his blind
        father off to the right.*]

THE BIG BOAST

Henry the Fourth, Part I. act II, scene 4

PRINCE HAL

FALSTAFF

POINS

A TAVERN BOY

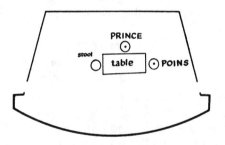

*A room in the Boar's Head Tavern
at Eastcheap*

INTRODUCTION. King Henry is having difficulties within his kingdom. He has aroused the enmity of certain of his noblemen and his throne is being threatened. Prince Hal, the son of King Henry, has taken no part in this quarrel. He has shown himself to be just a carefree lad who devotes his efforts to enjoying him-

89

self in the company of fat old Sir John Falstaff and other rogues. They all have just come from doing a bit of rascality as highwaymen. In the midst of it, Hal cleverly double-crossed Falstaff. In Boar's Head Tavern now, the Prince and one of his aides, Poins, are laughing over the mischief and drinking as Falstaff enters.

[*Prince Hal is seated behind the table with his companion, Poins, at his left.*]

FALSTAFF
[*Entering from the right.*]
A plague of* all cowards, I say, and a vengeance too!
[*He lowers himself onto the stool at the right of the table. A boy comes into the room from the left with cups of wine.*]

Marry,† and amen! Give me a cup of sack, boy. Ere I lead this life long, I'll sew nether stocks,‡ and mend them and foot them§ too. A plague of all cowards! Give me a cup of sack, rogue. Is there no virtue extant?
[*The boy who has been hesitating at the door quickly gives Falstaff the wine and goes out. Falstaff drinks thirstily.*]

* *a plague of:* a plague on
† *Marry:* a corruption of "by the Virgin Mary," an oath or (here) a light interjection   ‡ *nether stocks:* stockings
§ *foot them:* put new bottoms on them (That is, he's so disgusted, he's ready to be a stocking maker and mender.)

PRINCE
[*Looking at Falstaff and speaking to Poins.*]
Didst thou never see Titan* kiss a dish of butter,
pitiful-hearted Titan, that† melted at the sweet tale
of the sun?
[*Laughing and pointing at the fat old man.*]
If thou didst, then behold that compound.

FALSTAFF
You rogue, here's lime in this sack too.
[*Slamming the cup down on the table.*]
There is nothing but roguery to be found in villainous man; yet a coward is worse than a cup of sack
with lime in it. A villainous coward!
[*With a big noisy sigh.*]
Go thy ways, old Jack; die when thou wilt, if manhood, good manhood, be not forgot upon the face
of the earth, then am I a shotten† herring. There
lives not three good men unhang'd in England; and
one of them is fat and grows old. God help the
while!‡ a bad world, I say. I would I were a weav-
er; I could sing psalms or anything.
[*He roars out his disgust again.*]
A plague of all cowards, I say still.

PRINCE
How now, woolsack! what mutter you?

* *Titan:* Hyperion, the Sun   † *that:* the butter (The Prince
is referring to Falstaff's sweaty appearance.)
† *shotten:* having spawned   ‡ *the while:* the times

FALSTAFF
[*Glaring at the Prince.*]
A king's son! If I do not beat thee out of thy kingdom with a dagger of lath, and drive all thy subjects afore thee like a flock of wild geese, I'll never wear hair on my face more. You Prince of Wales!

PRINCE
[*Pretending innocence.*]
Why, you whoreson round man, what's the matter?

FALSTAFF
Are not you a coward? Answer me to that. You are straight enough in the shoulders; you care not who sees your back. Call you that backing of your friends? A plague upon such backing! Give me them that will face me.
[*Yelling for the tavern boy.*]
Give me a cup of sack. I am a rogue, if I drunk* today.

PRINCE
O villain! thy lips are scarce wip'd since thou drunk'st last.
[*The boy comes in with another cup of wine and hands it to Falstaff.*]

FALSTAFF
All's one for that.†
[*He gulps the wine, then bursts out again.*]
A plague of all cowards, still say I.

---

* *drunk:* have had a drop of drink
† *All's one for that:* it doesn't make any difference

PRINCE
What's the matter?

FALSTAFF
What's the matter! There be four of us here have ta'en a thousand pound this day morning.

PRINCE
[*Rising, as if he were delighted.*]
Where is it, Jack? where is it?

FALSTAFF
Where is it! Taken from us it is; a hundred upon* poor four of us.

PRINCE
[*Swinging around to the right of Falstaff in mock amazement.*]
What, a hundred, man?

FALSTAFF
I am a rogue, if I were not at half-sword† with a dozen of them two hours together. I have scaped by miracle. I am eight times thrust through the doublet, four through the hose; my buckler cut through and through; my sword hack'd like a handsaw—
[*He illustrates the encounters with gestures.*]
ecce signum!‡ I never dealt better since I was a man.
[*He shows his hacked-up sword.*]

---

* *a hundred upon:* a hundred men attacking
† *half-sword:* at close quarters ‡ *ecce signum:* behold the proof

PRINCE
What, fought you with them all?

FALSTAFF
All! I know not what you call all; but if I fought not with fifty of them, I am a bunch of radish. If there were not two or three and fifty upon poor old Jack, then I am no two-legg'd creature.

PRINCE
[*With pretended horror.*]
Pray God you have not murd'red some of them.

FALSTAFF
Nay, that's past praying for; I have pepper'd* two of them. Two I am sure I have paid,† two rogues in buckram suits. I tell thee what, Hal, if I tell thee a lie, spit in my face, call me horse. Thou knowest my old ward;‡ here I lay,
　　　[*He sprawls sideways on the table, raising and swinging his sword with his right hand.*]
and thus I bore my point. Four rogues in buckram let drive at me—

PRINCE
[*More and more impressed. He is still standing at Falstaff's right.*]
What, four? Thou saidst but two even now.

FALSTAFF
Four, Hal; I told thee four.

* *peppered:* pierced with my sword
† *paid:* paid off, killed   ‡ *ward:* posture of defence

POINS
[*Laughing.*]
Ay, ay, he said four.

FALSTAFF
These four came all a-front, and mainly* thrust at
me. I made me no more ado but took all their
seven points in my target,† thus.

PRINCE
Seven? why, there were but four even now.

FALSTAFF
In buckram?

POINS
Ay, four, in buckram suits.

FALSTAFF
[*Insisting on the number.*]
Seven, by these hilts, or I am a villain else.

PRINCE
[*Giving up, laughing.*]
Prithee, let him alone; we shall have more anon.

FALSTAFF
Dost thou hear me, Hal?

PRINCE
Ay, and mark‡ thee too, Jack.

* *mainly:* powerfully   † *target:* shield
‡ *mark:* follow your arithmetic

FALSTAFF

Do so, for it is worth the listening to. These nine in buckram that I told thee of—

PRINCE

So, two more already.

FALSTAFF

Their points* being broken—

POINS

Down fell their hose.

FALSTAFF
[*Getting on his feet.*]

Began to give me ground; but I followed me close, came in foot and hand, and with a thought seven of the eleven I paid.

PRINCE

O monstrous! eleven buckram men grown out of two!

FALSTAFF

But, as the devil would have it, three misbegotten knaves in Kendal green came at my back and let drive at me; for it was so dark, Hal, that thou couldst not see thy hand.

PRINCE
[*Laughing now as if he would burst.*]

These lies are like their father that begets them; gross as a mountain, open, palpable. Why thou

---

* *points:* points of swords (Points are also the laces which hold up stockings. This is the meaning Poins chooses to take.)

clay-brain'd guts, thou knotty-pated fool, thou whoreson, obscene, greasy tallow-catch—*

FALSTAFF
[*Acting as if he were deeply offended.*]
What, art thou mad? art thou mad? Is not the truth the truth?

PRINCE
Why, how couldst thou know these men in Kendal green, when it was so dark thou couldst not see thy hand? Come, tell us your reason; what say'st thou to this?

POINS
Come, your reason, Jack, your reason.

FALSTAFF
What, upon compulsion? 'Zounds, an† I were at the strappado,‡ or all the racks in the world, I would not tell you on compulsion. Give you a reason on compulsion! If reasons were as plenty as blackberries, I would give no man a reason upon compulsion, I.

PRINCE
I'll be no longer guilty of this sin.§ This sanguine coward, this bed-presser, this horseback-breaker, this huge hill of flesh—

FALSTAFF
'Sblood, you starveling, you elf-skin, you dried

---

* *tallow-catch* tallow tub   †*an:* if
‡ *strappado:* a form of Spanish torture   § *sin:* sin of deceit

neat's* tongue, you stockfish! † O for breath to utter what is like thee! you tailor's-yard, you sheath, you bowcase, you vile standing-tuck—‡

PRINCE
[*Patting the enraged, sputtering Falstaff on the back.*]
Well, breathe a while, and then to it again; and when thou hast tired thyself in base comparisons, hear me speak but this:—

POINS
Mark,§ Jack.

PRINCE
We two saw you four set on four and bound them, and were masters of their wealth. Mark now, how a plain tale shall put you down. Then did we two** set on you four; and, with a word, outfac'd†† you from your prize, and have it, yea, and can show it you here in the house; and, Falstaff, you carried your guts away as nimbly, with as quick dexterity, and roar'd for mercy, and still run and roar'd, as ever I heard bull-calf.
[*Laughing again.*]
What a slave art thou, to hack thy sword as thou hast done, and then say it was in fight! What trick, what device, what starting-hole,‡‡ canst thou now find out to hide thee from this open and apparent shame?

---

* *neat's:* ox's   † *stockfish:* dried cod
‡ *standing tuck:* a rapier standing on its point   § *mark:* listen
** *we two:* the Prince and Poins   †† *outfaced:* frightened
‡‡ *starting-hole:* evasion

POINS

Come, let's hear, Jack; what trick hast thou now?
[*Falstaff looks at one, then the other, then grins.*]

FALSTAFF

By the Lord, I knew ye as well as he that made ye. Why, hear you, my masters. Was it for me to kill the heir apparent? Should I turn upon the true Prince? Why, thou knowest I am as valiant as Hercules; but beware* instinct; the lion will not touch the true prince. Instinct is a great matter; I was now a coward on instinct. I shall think the better of myself and thee during my life; I for a valiant lion, and thou for a true prince.
[*Taking a long breath and sitting down.*]
But, by the Lord, lads. I am glad you have the money.
[*Calling into the room at the left.*]
Hostess, clap to the doors! Watch tonight, pray tomorrow.
[*Now to the two in the room.*]
Gallants, lads, boys, hearts of gold, all the titles of good fellowship come to you! What, shall we be merry? Shall we have a play extempore?

PRINCE
[*Going back to his seat behind the table.*]
Content; and the argument shall be thy running away.

FALSTAFF

Ah, no more of that, Hal, an thou lovest me!

_____

* *beware:* give head to

TURNABOUT

Henry the Fourth, Part I. act II, scene 4

PRINCE HAL

FALSTAFF

POINS

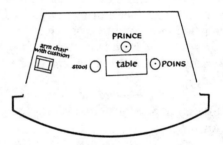

*A room in the Boar's Head Tavern
at Eastcheap*

INTRODUCTION. Falstaff has recounted the tale of his escapade to Prince Hal and Poins in the Boar's Head Tavern, and has twisted the story to his own credit. A nobleman of the court comes to the door and while Falstaff is talking to him outside the room, Prince Hal and Poins laugh over the merry prank and Falstaff.

[*Prince Hal and Poins are still seated at the table. Falstaff comes lumbering in from the right.*]

PRINCE

Here comes lean Jack, here comes bare-bone. How now, my sweet creature of bombast!* How long is't ago, Jack, since thou sawest thine own knee?

FALSTAFF
[*Trying to look down over his fat stomach at his knees.*]

My own knee? When I was about thy years, Hal, I was not an† eagle's talon in the waist; I could have crept into any alderman's thumb-ring.

[*Sitting down at the right of the table with a sigh.*]

A plague of‡ sighing and grief! it blows a man up like a bladder.

[*Now changing his tone to one of seriousness.*]

There's villainous news abroad. Here was Sir John Bracy from your father; you must to the court in the morning. That same mad fellow of the north, Percy, and he of Wales§ that gave Amamon** the

* *bombast:* cotton stuffing or padding
† *not an:* not more than   ‡ *a plague of:* a plague on
§ *he of Wales:* Owen Glendower, a Welsh warrior against whom the English have been fighting unsuccessfully
** *Amamon:* a devil

bastinado and made Lucifer cuckold and swore the devil his true liegeman upon the cross of a Welsh hook*—what a plague call you him?

POINS
O, Glendower.

FALSTAFF
Owen, Owen, the same; and his son-in-law Mortimer, and old Northumberland, and that sprightly Scot of Scots, Douglas, that runs o't horseback up a hill perpendicular—

PRINCE
[*Pretending to be awestruck like Falstaff.*]
He that rides at high speed and with his pistol kills a sparrow flying.

FALSTAFF
You have hit it.

PRINCE
[*Changing his tone.*]
So did he never the sparrow.

FALSTAFF
Well, that rascal hath good mettle in him; he will not run.

PRINCE
[*Rising.*]
Why, what a rascal art thou then, to praise him so for running!

* *Welsh hook:* a weapon with a curved blade   † *o':* on

FALSTAFF

O' horseback, ye cuckoo; but afoot he will not budge a foot.

PRINCE
[Jokingly reminding the old man of what he said about running in the last scene.]
Yes, Jack, upon instinct.

FALSTAFF

I grant ye, upon instinct. Well, he is there too, and one Murdoch, and a thousand bluecaps* more. Worcester is stolen away tonight. Thy father's beard is turn'd white with the news. You may buy land now as cheap as stinking mackerel.

PRINCE
[Walking around down left, below Poins.]
Why, then, it is like,† if there come a hot June and this civil buffeting hold,‡ we shall buy maidenheads as they buy hobnails, by the hundreds.

FALSTAFF

But tell me, Hal, art not thou horrible afeard? Thou being heir apparent, could the world pick thee out three such enemies again as that fiend Douglas, that spirit Percy, and that devil Glendower? Art thou not horribly afraid? Doth not thy blood thrill§ at it?

---

* *bluecaps:* Scots, who wore caps of blue wool
† *like:* likely   ‡ *hold:* continues   § *thrill:* tremble

PRINCE

Not a whit, i' faith; I lack some of thy instinct.

FALSTAFF

Well, thou wilt be horribly chid tomorrow when thou comest to thy father. If thou love me, practise an answer.

PRINCE
[*Turning.*]

Do thou stand for my father, and examine me upon the particulars of my life.

FALSTAFF
[*Getting up and going over to the right to the chair with the cushion.*]

Shall I? Content. This chair shall be my state, this dagger my scepter, and this cushion my crown.

PRINCE
[*Coming center, below the table, and surveying Falstaff in the chair.*]

Thy state is taken for a join'd-stool,* thy golden scepter for a leaden dagger, and thy precious rich crown for a pitiful bald crown!

FALSTAFF

Well, an† the fire of grace be not quite out of thee, now shalt thou be moved.‡ Give me a cup of sack to make my eyes look red, that it may be thought

---

* *join'd-stool:* a jointed wooden stool   † *an:* if
‡ *moved:* affected by emotion

I have wept; for I must speak in passion.

> [*The Prince hands him the cup from the table. Then he moves the stool out of the way and kneels in front of Falstaff, right of the table.*]

PRINCE
Well, here is my leg.

FALSTAFF
[*Assuming the dignified tone of the King.*]
Harry, I do not only marvel where thou spendest thy time, but also how thou art accompanied; for though the camomile, the more it is trodden on the faster it grows, yet youth, the more it is wasted the sooner it wears. That thou art my son, I have partly thy mother's word, partly my own opinion, but chiefly a villainous trick of thine eye and a foolish hanging of thy nether lip, that doth warrant* me. If then thou be son to me, here lies the point; why, being son to me, art thou so pointed at? Shall the blessed sun of heaven prove a micher† and eat blackberries? a question not to be ask'd. Shall the son of England prove a thief and take purses? a question to be ask'd. There is a thing, Harry, which thou hast often heard of and it is known to many in our land by the name of pitch. This pitch, as ancient writers do report, doth defile; so doth the company thou keepest; for, Harry, now I do not

* *warrant:* assure   † *micher:* truant

speak to thee in drink but in tears; not in pleasure but in passion, not in words only, but in woes also; and yet there is a virtuous man whom I have often noted in thy company, but I know not his name.

PRINCE
What manner of man, an it like your Majesty?

FALSTAFF
A goodly portly man, i' faith, and a corpulent; of a cheerful look, a pleasing eye, and a most noble carriage; and, as I think, his age some fifty, or, by 'r lady, inclining to threescore; and now I remember me, his name is Falstaff. If that man should be lewdly given,* he deceiveth me; for, Harry, I see virtue in his looks. If then the tree may be known by the fruit, as the fruit by the tree, then, peremptorily I speak it, there is virtue in that Falstaff; him keep with, the rest banish. And tell me now, thou naughty varlet,† tell me, where hast thou been this month?

PRINCE
[Getting up.]
Dost thou speak like a king? Do thou stand for me, and I'll play my father.

FALSTAFF
[Rising.]
Depose me? If thou dost it half so gravely, so

* given: inclined   † varlet: rascal

majestically, both in word and matter, hang me up
by the heels for a rabbit-sucker* or a poulter's
hare.
> [*The Prince sits in the chair and Falstaff
> takes his place in front of it.*]

PRINCE
Well, here I am set.

FALSTAFF
And here I stand. Judge, my masters.

PRINCE
[*Now speaking as the King.*]
Now, Harry, whence come you?

FALSTAFF
[*Imitating the Prince's voice.*]
My noble lord, from Eastcheap.

PRINCE
The complaints I hear of thee are grievous.

FALSTAFF
'Sblood,† my lord, they are false. Nay. I'll tickle
ye for a young prince, i' faith.

PRINCE
Swearest thou, ungracious boy? Henceforth ne'er
look on me. Thou art violently carried away from
grace. There is a devil haunts thee in the likeness

---

* *rabbit-sucker:* young rabbit
† *'Sblood:* from "God's blood," an interjection

of an old fat man; a tun of man is thy companion. Why dost thou converse with that trunk of humors, that bolting-hutch* of beastliness, that swollen parcel of dropsies, that huge bombard† of sack; that stuff'd cloak-bag of guts, that roasted Manningtree ox with the pudding in his belly, that reverend vice, that gray iniquity, that father ruffian, that vanity in years? Wherein is he good, but to taste sack and drink it? wherein neat and cleanly, but to carve a capon and eat it? wherein cunning, but in craft? wherein crafty, but in villainy? wherein villainous, but in all things? wherein worthy, but in nothing?

FALSTAFF

I would your Grace would take me with you.‡ Whom means your Grace?

PRINCE

That villainous abominable misleader of youth, Falstaff, that old white-bearded Satan.

FALSTAFF
[*Pretending to be surprised at this evaluaof Falstaff.*]

My lord, the man I know.

PRINCE

I know thou dost.

* *bolting-hutch:* miller's chest
† *bombard:* large leather vessel for liquor
‡ *take me with you:* explain to me what you mean

FALSTAFF

But to say I know more harm in him than in myself, were to say more than I know. That he is old, the more the pity, his white hairs do witness it. If to be old and merry be a sin, then many an old host that I know is damn'd. If to be fat be to be hated, then Pharaoh's lean kine are to be loved. No, my good lord; banish Peto, banish Bardolph, banish Poins, but for sweet Jack Falstaff, kind Jack Falstaff, true Jack Falstaff, valiant Jack Falstaff, and therefore more valiant, being, as he is, old Jack Falstaff, banish not him thy Harry's company, banish not him thy Harry's company. Banish plump Jack, and banish all the world.

PRINCE

I do, I will.

A MIGHTY CHARGE

Henry the Fifth. act III, scene 1

KING HENRY

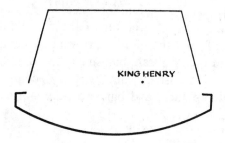

A field in front of the city of Harfleur

INTRODUCTION. Young King Henry, as a prince, was a light-hearted playboy. Now he is eager to establish himself as a strong and responsible king. The archbishop of Canterbury has assured him that by a certain interpretation of the "Salic law" Henry should by right be King of France as well as of England. So Henry with his army is fighting to establish his rule on the Continent. His cannoneers have breached the walls around the French city, Harfleur, and standing before his soldiers, he is preparing their spirits for a mighty charge through the breaks into the city.

KING HENRY
Once more unto the breach, dear friends, once
    more,*
Or close the wall up with our English dead.
In peace there's nothing so becomes a man†
As modest stillness and humility;
            [*His voice hardening as he begins to talk
            about the state of fighting.*]
But when the blast of war blows in our ears,
Then imitate the action of the tiger;
Stiffen the sinews, summon up the blood,
Disguise fair nature with hard-favor'd rage;
            [*His voice rising.*]
Then lend the eye a terrible aspect;
Let it pry through the portage of the head‡
Like the brass cannon; let the brow o'erwhelm it§
As fearfully as doth a galled rock**
O'erhang and jutty his confounded base,††
Now set the teeth and stretch the nostril wide,
Hold hard the breath, and bend up every spirit
To his full height. On, on, you noblest English,
Whose blood is fet from fathers of war-proof!‡‡
Fathers that, like so many Alexanders,
Have in these parts from morn till even fought,
And sheath'd their swords for lack of argument.§§
Dishonor not your mothers; now attest

---

* *breach:* break in the wall   † *so becomes:* is so suitable to
‡ *portage:* portholes, eye sockets   § *o'erwhelm:* overhang
** *galled:* worn away   †† *jutty:* project over   *confounded:*
wasted away   ‡‡ *fet:* fetched   §§ *argument:* cause of quarrel

That those whom you call'd fathers did beget you.
Be copy now to men of grosser blood,*
And teach them how to war.
                    [*Turning a little now as if he were ad-
                    dressing a different group.*]
                              And you, good yeomen,
Whose limbs were made in England, show us here
The mettle of your pasture; let us swear†
That you are worth your breeding, which I doubt
    not;
For there is none of you so mean and base
That hath not noble luster in your eyes.
                    [*Smiling proudly at his followers.*]
I see you stand like greyhounds in the slips,
Straining upon the start. The game's afoot!‡
Follow your spirit, and upon this charge
Cry, "God for Harry! England and Saint George!"

---

* *copy:* models (worth copying)   *grosser:* inferior
† *mettle of your pasture:* the stern nature of the land that has
nurtured you.   ‡ *straining upon the start:* eager to start running

ON CRISPIN'S DAY

Henry the Fifth. act IV, scene 3

GLOUCESTER

BEDFORD

WESTMORELAND

EXETER   KING HENRY

SALISBURY   MONTJOY

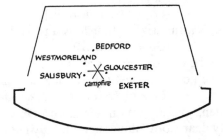

The English camp on the field of Agincourt

INTRODUCTION. In spite of the fall of Harfleur the French are very certain that they can defeat King Henry's "beggar'd soldiers," whom they despise. The battle about to be fought should decide the issue. The English are feeling none too confident of their chances of success against the superior French forces. Several

113

officers are standing and sitting around a fire in the English camp discussing the coming fight.

GLOUCESTER
Where is the King?

BEDFORD
The King himself is rode to view their battle.*

WESTMORELAND
Of fighting men they have full threescore thousand.

EXETER
[*Shaking his head sadly.*]
There's five to one; besides, they all are fresh.

SALISBURY
[*Fervently, as he rises.*]
God's arm strike with us! 'tis a fearful odds.
[*Going to the right.*]
God be wi' you, princes all; I'll to my charge.
If we no more meet till we meet in heaven,
[*Coming back to take their hands.*]
Then, joyfully, my noble Lord of Bedford,
My dear Lord Gloucester, and my good Lord Exeter,
[*He waves his hand at Exeter and turns to Westmoreland.*]
And my kind kinsman, warriors all, adieu!

BEDFORD
Farewell, good Salisbury, and good luck go with thee!

* *their battle:* the French troops

EXETER
[*Stepping in.*]
Farewell, kind lord; fight valiantly today!
And yet I do thee wrong to mind thee of it,
For thou art fram'd of the firm truth of valor.*
          [*Salisbury goes out right.*]

BEDFORD
He is as full of valor as of kindness,
Princely in both.
          [*The King comes in from the left. He nods
          at Exeter as he passes him on the way to
          the fire. Gloucester gets up.*]

WESTMORELAND
               O that we now had here
But one ten thousand of those men in England
That do no work today!
          [*The King, who has been warming his
          hands at the fire, turns to his officers.*]

KING HENRY
What's he that wishes so?
My cousin Westmoreland? No, my fair cousin.
If we are mark'd to die, we are enow†
To do our country loss; and if to live,
The fewer men, the greater share of honor.
God's will! I pray thee, wish not one man more.
          [*Walking strongly past Exeter to the left.*]
By Jove, I am not covetous for gold,

* *fram'd:* constructed   † *enow:* enough

Nor care I who doth feed upon my cost;
It yearns me not if men my garments wear;*
Such outward things dwell not in my desires;
        [*Turning his head toward his companions.*]
But if it be a sin to covet honor
I am the most offending soul alive.
No, 'faith, my coz, wish not a man from England.†
        [*Walking back to the fire and looking
        Westmoreland straight in the face.*]
God's peace! I would not lose so great an honor
As one man more, methinks, would share from
    me‡
For the best hope I have. O, do not wish one more!
Rather proclaim it, Westmoreland, through my
    host,
That he which hath no stomach to this fight,
Let him depart.
        [*Looking out into the night thoughtfully.*]
This day is call'd the feast of Crispian.
He that outlives this day and comes safe home
Will stand a tiptoe when this day is named,
And rouse him at the name of Crispian.§
He that shall live this day, and see old age,
Will yearly on the vigil feast his neighbors,
And say, "Tomorrow is Saint Crispian."
        [*His voice rising steadily in strength.*]
Then will he strip his sleeve and show his scars,

* *yearns:* grieves
† *coz:* cousin   ‡ *share from me:* take from me by sharing
§ *rouse him:* lift his head high in pride

And say, "These wounds I had on Crispin's day."
This story shall the good man teach his son;
And Crispin Crispian shall ne'er go by,
From this day to the ending of the world,
          [*Turning around to look at his compan-
          ions.*]
But we in it shall be remembered,
We few, we happy few, we band of brothers.
          [*Salisbury comes back in from the right.*]

SALISBURY
My sovereign lord, bestow yourself with speed.*
The French are bravely in their battles set,
And will with all expedience charge on us.

KING HENRY
All things are ready, if our minds be so.

WESTMORELAND
[*Stepping down, around the fire to the
King's side.*]
Perish the man whose mind is backward now!

KING HENRY
[*Turning to him, smiling affectionately.*]
Thou dost not wish more help from England, coz?

WESTMORELAND
[*Taking the King's hand firmly.*]
God's will! my liege, would you and I alone,
Without more help, could fight this royal battle!

* *bestow yourself:* take your position

KING HENRY
Why, now thou hast unwish'd five thousand men,
Which likes me better than to wish us one.
        [*Turning to the others.*]
You know your places. God be with you all!
        [*They start to scatter, but stop on the
        flourish of a trumpet. A French herald en-
        ters left.*]

MONTJOY
[*Insolently*]
Once more I come to know of thee, King Harry,
If for thy ransom thou wilt now compound,*
Before thy most assured overthrow;
For certainly thou art so near the gulf,†
Thou needs must be englutted. Besides, in mercy,‡
The Constable desires thee thou wilt mind§
Thy followers of repentance; that their souls
May make a peaceful and a sweet retire
From off these fields, where, wretches, their poor
    bodies
Must lie and fester.

KING HENRY
[*Feeling a rise of anger.*]
                    Who hath sent thee now?

MONTJOY
The Constable of France.

* *compound:* make terms   † *gulf:* whirlpool
‡ *Thou needs must be englutted:* you will surely be swallowed
§ *Constable:* a high officer of the French realm   *mind:* remind

KING HENRY
[*Loudly and strongly.*]
I pray thee, bear my former answer back:
Bid them achieve me and then sell my bones.*
Good God! why should they mock poor fellows
    thus?
The man that once did sell the lion's skin
While the beast liv'd, was kill'd with hunting him.
Let me speak proudly: tell the Constable
We are but warriors for the working-day.
Our gayness and our gilt are all besmirch'd†
With rainy marching in the painful field;
There's not a piece of feather in our host—‡
Good argument, I hope, we will not fly—§
And time hath worn us into slovenry;**
But, by the mass, our hearts are in the trim;
And my poor soldiers tell me, yet ere night
They'll be in fresher robes, or they will pluck
The gay new coats o'er the French soldiers' heads
And turn them out of service. If they do this—
As, if God please, they shall—my ransom then
Will soon be levied. Herald, save thou thy labor.
Come thou no more for ransom, gentle herald.
        [*The word "gentle" is said sarcastically.*]

        MONTJOY
I shall, King Harry. And so fare thee well;
Thou never shalt hear herald any more.
        [*He goes out left.*]

* *achieve:* capture, or kill   † *besmirch'd:* soiled
‡ *not a piece of feather:* no fancy warrior's decoration
§ *Good argument:* good reason why
** *slovenry:* the appearance of being slipshod

KING HENRY
[*Shouting after him.*]
I fear thou will once more come again for ransom.

[*York, another English officer, enters right.*]

YORK
[*Kneeling*]
My lord, most humbly on my knee I beg
The leading of the vaward,*

KING HENRY
Take it, brave York. Now, soldiers, march away;
[*Moving right.*]
And how thou pleasest, God, dispose the day!
[*He goes out and the others scatter, each to his own station.*]

* *vaward:* vanguard

WOOING IN TWO LANGUAGES

Henry the Fifth. act V, scene 2

KING HENRY

PRINCESS KATHARINE

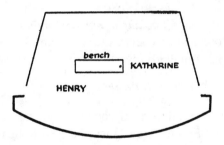

A room in the French royal palace

INTRODUCTION. Having beaten the French army and thus conquered their country, King Henry is eager to establish a close union between France and England. He persuades the French King to grant him the hand of fair Katharine. But Henry has yet to win the consent of the spirited Princess herself. In this scene the bluff English King tries awkwardly, by means of his limited French to persuade her that he loves her and wants her to be his Queen.

[*The Princess is seated on the bench and Henry is moving uneasily about, to the right of her.*]

KING HENRY
Fair Katharine, and most fair,
Will you vouchsafe to teach a soldier terms
Such as will enter at a lady's ear
And plead his love-suit to her gentle heart?

KATHARINE
[*Looking at him demurely.*]
Your Majesty shall mock at me: I cannot speak your England.

KING HENRY
[*Sitting beside her impulsively.*]
O fair Katharine, if you will love me soundly with your French heart, I will be glad to hear you confess it brokenly with your English tongue. Do you like me, Kate?

KATHARINE
Pardonnez-moi, I cannot tell wat is "like me."

KING HENRY
An angel is like you, Kate, and you are like an angel.

KATHARINE
O bon Dieu! les langues des hommes sont pleines de tromperies.

KING HENRY
[*Smiling*]
I am glad thou canst speak no better English; for,
if thou couldst, thou wouldst find me such a plain
king that thou wouldst think I had sold my farm to
buy my crown. I know no ways to mince it* in
love, but directly to say, "I love you"; then if you
urge me farther than to say, "Do you in faith?" I
wear out my suit.† Give me your answer; i' faith,
do; and so clap hands‡ and a bargain.
[*Leaning toward her fondly.*]
How say you, lady?

[*She laughs gaily.*]

KATHARINE
Sauf votre honneur, me understand well.

[*Henry gets up suddenly, knowing very
well that he is courting awkwardly but
not knowing what to do about it.*]

KING HENRY
Marry, if you would put me to verses, or to dance
for your sake, Kate, why you undid me. If I might
buffet§ for my love, or bound my horse** for her
favors.
[*Striding over to the right, then pretending
he is riding a horse and swinging a sword.*]

* *mince it:* act elegantly
† *wear out my suit:* run out of all the courting phrases I know
‡ *clap hands:* clasp hands (in agreement)
§ *buffet:* strike an enemy or contender with blows
** *bound my horse:* make my horse leap

I could lay on like a butcher and sit like a jack-an-apes,* never off.
> [*Stopping his clowning and turning to the Princess sadly.*]

But, before God, Kate, I cannot look greenly,† nor gasp out my eloquence.
> [*Crossing to her, behind the right end of the bench.*]

If thou canst love a fellow of this temper, Kate, whose face is not worth sunburning, that never looks in his glass for love of anything he sees there, let thine eye be thy cook.‡
> [*Putting a foot on the bench and bringing his face close to hers, appealingly.*]

What say'st thou to my love? Speak, my fair, and fairly, I pray thee.

KATHARINE
> [*With wide open eyes.*]

It is possible dat I should love de enemy of France?

KING HENRY
> [*Smiling again.*]

No; it is not possible you should love the enemy of France, Kate; but, in loving me, you should love the friend of France; for I love France so well that I will not part with a village of it, I will have it all

---

* *jack-an-apes:* monkey   *never off:* never falling off
† *greenly:* lovesick   ‡ *be thy cook:* add the garnishing

mine; and, Kate, when France is mine and I am yours, then yours is France and you are mine.
[*Sitting beside her with his legs on the other side of the bench.*]

KATHARINE
I cannot tell wat is dat.

KING HENRY
No, Kate? I will tell thee in French; which I am sure will hang upon my tongue like a new-married wife about her husband's neck, hardly to be shook off.
[*With great difficulty.*]
Je quand sur le possession de France, et quand vous avez le possession de moi—let me see, what then? Saint Denis be my speed!—*donc votre est France et vous êtes mienne.*
[*Getting up again, angry at himself for his inability to find the right words.*]
It is as easy for me, Kate, to conquer the kingdom as to speak so much more French.
[*Striding down right.*]
I shall never move thee in French, unless it be to laugh at me.

KATHARINE
[*In a very pretty tone of voice.*]
Sauf votre honneur, le Francais que vous parlez, il est meilleur que l'Anglais lequel je parle.

KING HENRY
[*Going back to her.*]
No, faith, is't not, Kate.
[*Sitting.*]
Dost thou understand thus much English: canst thou love me?

KATHARINE
[*Shaking her head mischievously.*]
I cannot tell.

KING HENRY
[*Becoming exasperated now.*]
Can any of your neighbors tell, Kate? I'll ask them.
[*Tentatively he puts an arm around her.*]
Come, I know thou lovest me; and at night, when you come into your closet,* you'll question this gentlewoman about me; and I know, Kate, you will to her dispraise those parts in me that you love with your heart. But, good Kate, mock me mercifully; the rather, gentle princess, because I love thee cruelly.
[*Taking her hand and holding it in his.*]
Come, your answer in broken music; for thy voice is music and thy English broken; therefore, queen of all, Katharine, break thy mind† to me in broken English. Wilt thou have me?

* *closet:* room   † *break thy mind:* open your mind

KATHARINE
[*Dropping her eyes modestly.*]
Dat is as it shall please de *roi mon pere.*

KING HENRY
Nay, it will please him well, Kate; it shall please
him, Kate.
[*She hesitates a moment, then smiles at
him.*]

KATHARINE
Den it sall also content me.

KING HENRY
Upon that I kiss your hand, and call you my queen.
[*He brings her hand to his lips.*]

KATHARINE
[*Pulling away—as a properly brought up
Princess should.*]
*Laissez, mon seigneur, laissez, laissez! Ma foi, je
ne veux point que vous abaissez votre grandeur en
baisant la main d'une de votre seigneurie indigne
serviteur. Excusez-moi, je vous supplie, mon très-
puissant seigneur.*

KING HENRY
[*Not letting her get away.*]
Then I will kiss your lips, Kate.

KATHARINE
[*Protesting—but not too much.*]
Les dames et demoiselles pour être baisées devant

leur noces, il n'est pas la coutume de France.

KING HENRY

O Kate, nice customs curtsy to great kings. You
and I cannot be confined within the weak list of a
country's fashion. We are the makers of manners,
Kate; therefore,

> [*Putting his arm around her again and
> drawing her gently to him.*]

patiently and yielding.

> [*They kiss. He draws a long breath at the
> end of it.*]

You have witchcraft in your lips, Kate; there is
more eloquence in a sugar touch of them than in
the tongues of the French council; and they should
sooner persuade Harry of England than a general
petition of monarchs.

SHADOW IN THE SUN

Richard the Third. act I, scene 1

RICHARD

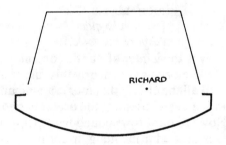

RICHARD

A quiet London street

INTRODUCTION. England has endured several frightful wars but now they are over and Edward the Fourth is King. While the members of the nobility and the common people, both, are rejoicing in the return of peace, one man is not happy. He is the humpbacked Richard, Duke of Gloucester and brother of Edward. Jealous of his brother's power, brooding on his own deformities, and restless because he has no outlet for his driving energies now that the fighting is finished, Richard is determined to play the villain. He uses as a means for his plotting an old prophecy that an individual whose name starts with "G" shall be the

129

murderer of the King's heirs. (It so happens that one of Edward's and Richard's brothers has the name of George.) Richard is standing in a quiet London street talking to himself. Since he refers bitterly in the following scene to his "shadow in the sun" we have chosen that phrase as the title for this selection.

RICHARD
[*He speaks quietly with just a note of sarcasm in his voice.*]
Now is the winter of our discontent
Made glorious summer by this sun of York;*
And all the clouds that lour'd upon our house
In the deep bosom of the ocean buried.
Now are our brows bound with victorious wreaths;
Our bruised arms hung up for monuments;†
Our stern alarums chang'd to merry meetings,‡
Our dreadful marches to delightful measures.
          [*Walking down left.*]
Grim-visag'd War hath smooth'd his wrinkled
     front;
And now, instead of mounting barbed steeds§
To fight the souls of fearful adversaries,
          [*Turning center as if he were watching a dance.*]
He capers nimbly in a lady's chamber

---

* *sun:* a play on both "son" and "sun" (He is referring to the new King, Edward IV.)   † *arms:* weapons
‡ *alarums:* calls to combat   § *barbed:* armed

To the lascivious pleasing of a lute.
> [*Now, as he crosses right, his voice changes*
> *to bitterness.*]

But I, that am not shap'd for sportive tricks,
Nor made to court an amorous looking-glass;
I, that am rudely stamp'd, and want love's majesty
To strut before a wanton ambling nymph;*
I, that am curtail'd of this fair proportion,
Cheated of feature by dissembling nature,†
Deform'd, unfinish'd, sent before my time
Into this breathing world, scarce half made up,
And that so lamely and unfashionable‡
That dogs bark at me as I halt by them;§
Why, I, in this weak piping time of peace,
Have no delight to pass away the time,
Unless to see my shadow in the sun
And descant on mine own deformity.**

> [*His voice hardening as he comes center*
> *and looks front.*]

And therefore, since I cannot prove a lover
To entertain these fair well-spoken days,
I am determined to prove a villain
And hate the idle pleasures of these days.

> [*More slily.*]

Plots have I laid, inductions dangerous,††
By drunken prophecies, libels, and dreams,

---

* *wanton:* playful   *nymph:* young girl
† *feature:* general appearance (Richard is hump-backed.)
dissembling: cheating   ‡ unfashionable: badly made
§ *halt:* limp
** *descant:* comment variously   †† *inductions:* preparations

[*Looking to the left as if his future victims
are off there somewhere.*]
To set my brother Clarence and the King
In deadly hate the one against the other;
[*Front again, with satisfaction.*]
And if King Edward be as true and just
As I am subtle, false, and treacherous,
This day should Clarence closely be mew'd up*
About a prophecy, which says that G
Of Edward's heirs the murderer shall be.
[*He chuckles a little to himself, then stops
and says the last line slowly and menac-
ingly.*]
Dive, thoughts, down to my soul!

* *mew'd:* caged